101 Favorite Freshwater FISH RECIPES

by Dr. Duane R. Lund

Distributed by

Adventure Publications
P.O. Box 269
Cambridge, MN 55008

Printed in the United States of America

2nd Printing 1981

3rd Printing 1982

4th Printing 1984

5th Printing 1985

6th Printing 1987

7th Printing 1989

8th Printing 1992

9th Printing 1994

10th Printing 1997

D1316669

*You will note some blank pages throughout this book.
These are for your notes.*

ISBN 0-934860-11-4

acknowledgements

This book has been prepared with help from the following consultants and their contributions are sincerely appreciated by the author:

Ed Morey, Founder of the Morey Fish Co. of Motley Brainerd, Minnesota.

Sally Killion and **Bruce Hayenga,** instructors in Chef Training Program of the Staples Area Vocational Technical Institute, Staples, Minnesota.

contents

introduction

For untold generations seafoods have been the subject of literally thousands of cookbooks and have been among the specialities of the world's leading chefs. Meanwhile, freshwater fish, because of their relative scarcity, have been largely ignored.

With the thousands of lakes and streams in the Upper Midwest and over most of Canada we have been blessed with a relative abundance of a great variety of freshwater fish. Not only are they available to fishermen, but they are netted commercially in the Great Lakes, Lake of the Woods and Lower Red Lake in Minnesota as well as in many parts of Canada, and are therefore available in the market place and at prices which are usually a little lower than comparable seafoods.

Generally speaking, freshwater fish are more tasty than their saltwater cousins and may be preserved much longer. The quality of fish, in general, tends to deteriorate from the moment they die—but the rate of deterioration for the saltwater varieties is much more rapid.

And so it is the purpose of this book to:

- Provide proven and tested recipes for your maximum enjoyment of freshwater fish,
- Describe the best techniques for cleaning and preserving all varieties, and
- Suggest ways of getting the most out of every fish caught or bought.

The major divisions of this book are separated by tables of time-tested tips for catching the more popular species.

So—read and enjoy!

chapter I

THE CARE, CLEANING AND PRESERVING OF FRESHWATER FISH

As stated in the Introduction, the quality of fish can deteriorate quite rapidly, so for maximum enjoyment—take proper care of your fish just as soon as each is caught (or bought). Here are some basic but important suggestions:

- A live box, live basket, or stringer are all fine for keeping fish in good condition—*but only as long as the fish stay healthy*; *never* tow dead fish around the lake or leave them floating belly-up in your live box. If you use a stringer, the steel-snap variety is excellent for walleyes and bass. Push the steel through both the upper and lower jaws to prevent drowning. Northerns or muskies will twist a steel snap open, so use a nylon rope-type stringer for them—again pushing the steel tip through both jaws. Never string a fish through the gills. A live basket is excellent for panfish.

  The best method is to carry a cooler of crushed ice and throw your fish in as you catch them.

- Even fish that are still alive but are in the process of dying are diminishing in quality.

- Fish fillets may be frozen in ice and kept for several months.

- Fillets or whole fish may be glazed with ice and kept for several weeks or as long as the ice seals in the quality. Air is the enemy; it dries out the fish and changes the flavor. For proper glazing—chill the fish; then submerge in ice water (with ice chunks or shavings floating in the water) then place them in the coldest part of your freezer. The more rapidly foods are frozen, the better. Repeat the process two or three times for a good glaze.

- Fillets or whole fish may be wrapped in foil or "freezer-wrap" and quick frozen for short periods of time (several weeks).
- Oily fish such as trout or whitefish do not keep well but quality may be substantially restored after thawing by soaking the fillets in milk for two or three hours.
- Smoked fish must be refrigerated for safe keeping. Freezing is not recommended but smoked fish may be frozen if you have too large a supply to consume over a couple of weeks. Frozen smoked fish should be thawed slowly—in a refrigerator.
- Frozen fish keep best at a constant temperature.

Fish cleaning techniques are important, both in terms of quality and reducing waste. Here are some practical suggestions:

- Choose your knife carefully; the blade should be relatively long (about 6 or 7 inches), narrow, and *slightly* flexible.
- To get the most possible meat, start your cut as near the gill covers as you can and finish the cut at the very tail itself. Slide the knife along the backbone so as not to waste any of the fish.
- Begin the operation by inserting the point of the blade (figure #1) immediately in back of the head and slightly off center so as to just miss the backbone. Follow the backbone towards the tail—cutting about halfway through the fish and going all the way through the body after you reach the vent-hole. (figure #2). Now make a vertical cut along the head, from top to bottom, following close to the gill cover. (figure #3).

  Grasp the loosened fillet at the head-end with your hand that is not holding the knife; as you pull the fillet away from the body, cut with the knife as necessary. (figure #4). Repeat the procedure on the other side of the fish. Now you should have both fillets free from the skeleton.

  If you happened to cut through the ribs in the process (some prefer to follow around the ribs), remove the rib cage from the fillet with the tip of your knife.

  Remove the skin by laying the fillet on a flat surface (figures #5 and #6), flesh side up—and then, starting at the tail end, separate the skin from the meat by sliding the knife flat against the skin and moving towards the head-end of the fillet, holding the tail-end of the skin with your fingers or a pliers and pulling on the skin as you push on the knife. It helps to pull the skin from one side to the other as you move the knife forward. Although the knife blade should be held flat, it will help if the cutting edge is slanted against the skin so as not to lose any meat.

You may want to leave the fillets attatched to the tail and then use the tail as a handle in the skinning process.

- Bass and northerns from warm or muddy waters may have a strong taste in the belly meat. If you suspect this may be the case, trim away that portion of the fillet.

DE-BONING NORTHERN PIKE FILLETS

- Northern pike fillets may be de-boned (completely). You will have to waste some meat—but it's well worth it. The process works best on fish over three pounds, but with practice you will be able to perform the "surgery" on smaller northerns.

(1) Fillet the northern the same as you would a walleye or any other fish. Leave the skin on the fillet until after you have finished the de-boning process.

(2) The ridge of meat containing the bones will be visible. Cut an "inverted V" along the sides of this ridge, but not all the way through the fillet, as shown in figure #7.

(3) Make a horizontal cut between the ends of the "V" at the large end of the fillet. Now lift the ridge of bones in one strip out of the fillet as you release it with your knife. (figures #8 and #9)

(4) Run your finger (carefully) down the cut; if you feel any "Y" bones left—remove them.

(5) Skin the fillet.

Smaller northerns may be deboned—quickly—by cutting off the tail piece (about ¼ of the fillet) which usually has few bones. Then make your "V cuts" all the way through the fillet. With this process it is better to remove the skin before you make the cuts just described. You will end up with two rather long, narrow fillets or "fish sticks," plus the tail piece.

- If the fillets from a large fish are too thick to fry well (especially if you like your fish crisp), try slicing the fillet in two—lengthwise, with a horizontal cut.

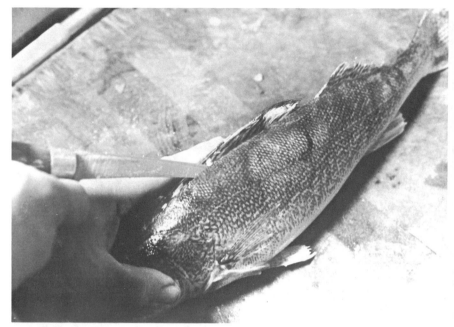

(Figure #1)

(Figure #2)

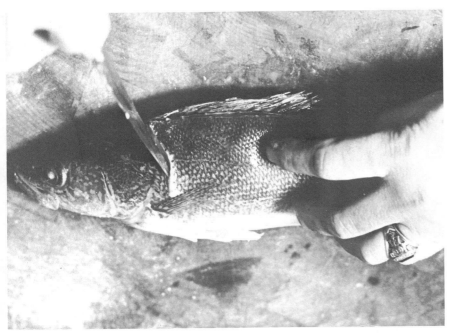

(Figure #3)

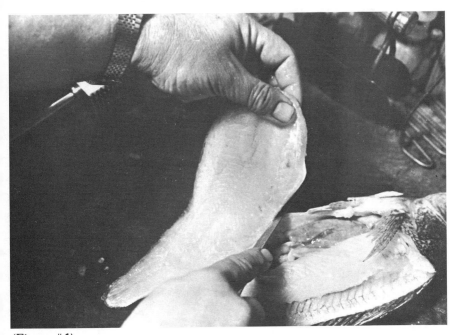

(Figure #4)

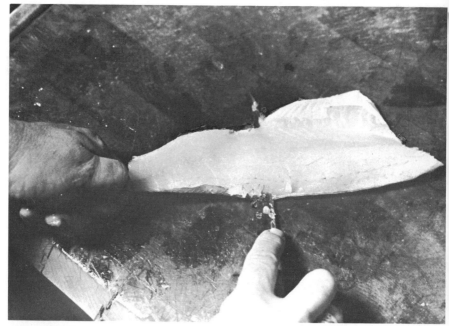

(Figure #5)

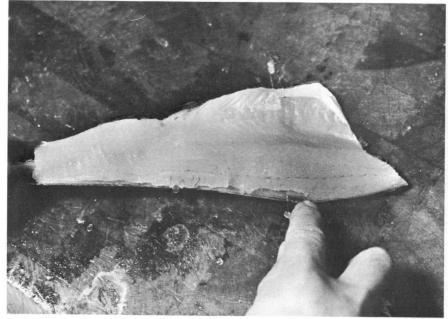

(Figure #6)

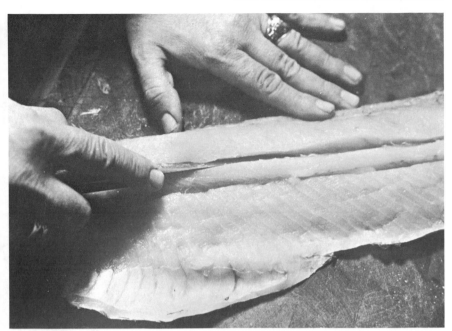

(Figure #7)

(Figure #8)

(Figure #9)

chapter II

FRIED FISH

Without a doubt, most people prefer their fish fried—at least most of the time. Perhaps no other technique brings out so much flavor. Here are some time-proven variations:

1 BASIC FRYING

This simple recipe is just about the best we have found for any "good eating" fillet. This includes walleye, northern pike, bass (from clear, northern waters), trout, sunfish, crappies, perch, eelpout, etc. Panfish may be filleted or fried whole.

You may roll your fillets in corn meal, flour, bread crumbs, dry cereal crumbs, or special preparations off your grocer's shelf—BUT *cracker crumbs are best.* Cracker crumbs do not detract from the flavor nor are they flavorless; they have just enough saltiness to enhance the taste.

Wash and dry the fillets (paper towels work well). If the fish are large, cut the fillets into pieces about six inches long or less so that they can be easily handled in the pan. If the fish is enormous, cut cross-section steaks about one-half to three-fourths of an inch thick.

Prepare the crumbs from ordinary soda crackers. Crush them fine—but not powdery. One-fourth pound of crackers will make enough crumbs for at least one pound of fillets. Place the crumbs in a bowl.

Beat an egg into a cup of water.[1] For more than one pound of fillets, use more eggs and more water (about one egg and one cup per pound).

[1]Some prefer milk, but burned milk has a scorched taste.

Preheat the griddle or frying pan over a medium-hot stove (more hot than medium). Use a generous covering of cooking oil (or butter, margarine, or bacon grease)—about ¼ inch. Add oil as it disappears. A couple of drops of water will spit and spatter when the griddle is ready.

Season both sides of the fillets with salt and pepper. You can be fairly generous with the seasoning because much of it will wash off in the next step, and that is: dip the fillets in the egg and milk mixture. Now dip the fillets in the cracker crumbs, making sure both sides are well covered. Lay the fillets in the preheated frying pan or on the hot griddle.

Fish will cook quickly; the fillets will be done when both sides are a deep brown—about seven or eight minutes on a side (depending on the heat).

When preparing large quantities of fish, fried fillets may be kept warm in the oven until all the fillets are ready. Fry the thick fillets first. Store them in a low oven (200°).

If you are using a frying pan, you can make sure your thick fillets are fully done by adding a couple of spoons of water and covering the pan for a minute or two. This process tends to take away the crispness, so continue to fry fish a couple of minutes on each side after you remove the cover.

In summary, for 2 lbs. of fillets you will need:

> one-third lb. cracker crumbs
> cooking oil or ½ lb. butter or margarine
> salt and pepper
> 2 eggs stirred into 2 cups of water

Serve your fried fish with tartar sauce and/or lemon wedges.

2 BUTTER FRIED FILLETS

An entirely different taste experience may be achieved by using butter or margarine. Use the above basic recipe but use medium heat and fry the fish slowly so that the fish and melted butter will not burn. When the griddle is ready, the butter will be "bubbly" all over. If the butter starts to turn dark brown this indicates that it is too hot and it will impart a burned taste to the fish.

Bacon grease will give your fish still another flavor. You may use more heat with bacon grease for crisp fillets.

Try adding a few spoons of bacon grease to cooking oil for an ideal combination.

3 DEEP FRIED FILLETS – IN BATTER

Fillets coated with a flour-egg batter and deep fried are very good and make an excellent change of pace.

Pour a third of a cup of beer[1] into a bowl and let sit overnight or until "flat." (Milk or water may be substituted for the beer)

Add the beer and a tablespoon of cooking oil to two cups of white flour. Mix. Beat the whites of three eggs until stiff and work them into the batter.

Dip the fillets into the batter and deep-fry in hot cooking oil (about 375°) until golden brown. The batter tends to insulate the fish so make sure they are well done before serving.

(For an extra crispiness, fold in a cup of wheaties or other dry cereal as the final step in preparing the batter[2])

4 DEEP FRIED FILLETS – PANCAKE BATTER[3]

Using a package pancake mix, prepare the batter exactly as you would for making pancakes (but not too heavy). Dip the fillets— without seasoning—and deep fry at 375°.

5 DEEP FRIED FISH AND TATERS[4]

Here is a proven favorite that makes it possible to prepare your fish and potatoes in the same kettle—making it easier to cook a meal on that small camp stove. But it will taste so good you'll find yourself preparing "fish and taters" at home—the same way.

For the batter, combine the following ingredients, mix thoroughly:

1 beaten egg
½ cup milk
¾ cup flour
dash of salt
1 tablespoon melted butter or margarine

Preheat two quarts of cooking oil in a deep iron skillet or kettle to 375°. Slice potatoes 3/8" thick (skins included if you wish). Dip the seasoned fish fillets in batter and fry in the oil for about 30 seconds or until slightly brown before adding the potatoes. If the fillets are thick, remove the potato slices before the fish is done to prevent overcooking. Turn the fillets and potatoes frequently to insure uniform cooking. If oil retains 375° temperature and the fillets are

---

[1] If you are a "tea-totaller" don't worry about alcoholic content; it will evaporate in the frying process.
[2] Courtesy Neil Krough, Staples, Minnesota.
[3] Courtesy Earl Mergens, Staples, Minnesota.
[4] Courtesy Jim Vogel, Staples, Minnesota.

not too thick, fish and "chips" should be done in 7-9 minutes cooking time. Serve with another vegetable and toast.

It is important that the oil be just the right temperature; therefore, you are strongly urged to bring along a thermometer (the kind that fits over the edge of the pan or kettle).

6 DEEP FRIED—CAPE COD BATTER

Season the fish fillets with salt and lemon-pepper.[1]

Marinate 2# of fillets for one hour by pouring the following solution over the fish:

> 5 tablespoons cooking oil or olive oil
> 4 tablespoons white wine
> 4 tablespoons lemon juice

Now, slice an onion—thin—and lay these slices on the fillets while they are in the marinade.

Meanwhile, make a batter of 2 cups of flour, two eggs, and two cups of milk. Add more (or less) milk to achieve the consistency you normally prefer.

After one hour of marinating, remove the fillets and cut into serving size pieces and drain on a paper towel.

Dip the fillets in the batter and deep-fry in pre-heated oil until well browned.

7 FRIED ALASKA[2]

Cut the fish fillets into strips 1½" x 2" in size. Salt, pepper, and paprika the strips and dust on all sides with pancake mix. (This can be done ahead of time but lay the strips in such a way that they do not touch each other or they will become moist.

Mix enough white wine or cooking sherry with pancake mix to make a thin batter.

Heat one half inch of oil in a heavy skillet to 350°. Dip strips in batter and fry on both sides until brown.

This recipe is especially good with fillets from larger fish—which normally are hard to fry because they are so thick. Lake trout, fresh salmon, and walleyes are prime candidates for this technique.

---

[1]Use ordinary ground, black pepper if not available.
[2]Courtesy Mrs. Paul Carlson, Port Alsworth, Alaska.

8 OVEN-FRIED FISH

Season the fillets (salt and lemon-pepper).

Prepare a batter of egg and water. Stir one egg into one cup of water for each pound of fish.

Dip the fillets in the water-egg mixture and roll in cracker crumbs (or bread crumbs, crushed corn flakes, or corn meal).

Bake in 500° oven (very hot) on a greased cookie sheet for about fifteen minutes.

9 FRYING OVER AN OPEN CAMPFIRE

Most everything tastes better out-of-doors. This is especially true of fresh-caught fish.

Use a heavy iron frying pan or griddle—balanced on rocks or on a grill over the fire.

Let the fire die down a bit so that the flames will not lick their way into the pan. If you have time, wait for the coals to form.

Use a generous portion of cooking oil. (It is hard to keep butter or margarine from burning over an open fire.)

If you are "traveling light," you may use flour to coat the seasoned fish—or—carry the flour in a paper bag with salt and pepper already added. Then, just shake the fillets in the bag and they are ready to fry. But if you can bring an egg along without breaking it, stir it into a cup of water. Dip the seasoned fillets into the egg-water mixture and then roll in cracker crumbs (or whatever) and fry until brown on both sides.

Fish that is not going to be dipped in a batter such as egg and water should not be seasoned as heavily as fillets which will be dipped. A certain amount of seasoning always washes off.

10 FRESHWATER FILLETS with ALMONDS

A gourmet sensation—

Ingredients:
   2 eggs
   1 tablespoon milk
   1½ lb. perch or pike fillets, cut into serving pieces
   ½ teaspoon salt
   Freshly ground black pepper
   ½ cup flour
   1 cup almonds, pulverized in a blender or with a nut grinder
   4 tablespoons butter
   2 tablespoons vegetable oil
   2 lemons, each cut lengthwise into quarters

In a small shallow bowl, beat the eggs lightly with a whisk or table fork and mix in the milk. Pat the fish completely dry with paper towels and sprinkle with the salt and a few grindings of pepper. Spread the flour on one piece of wax paper and the nuts on another. Dip the fillets in the flour, then shake gently to remove the excess. One at a time, immerse the fillets in the egg mixture and then place them on the nuts, turning them over until they are evenly coated on both sides. Arrange the fillets in one layer on wire cake racks set over a cookie sheet. Refrigerate for at least 30 minutes. When you are ready to fry the fish, melt the butter with the oil in a heavy 10-12 inch skillet over moderate heat. When the foam begins to subside, add 3 or 4 fillets, depending on their size. Fry the fillets for 3 to 5 minutes on each side turning them with a spatula. When done they should be crisp and brown and feel firm to the touch. Transfer to a heated platter and garnish with the quartered lemons.

11 FRIED FISH WITH TOMATO AND EGG SAUCE

A whole new taste treat!

Ingredients:

1 to 1½ lbs. fish fillets cut crosswise into 1 inch thick steaks
1 tablespoon plus 1 teaspoon salt
1 cup plus 2 tablespoons vegetable oil
1 teaspoon finely chopped garlic
⅓ cup coarsely chopped onions
1 tomato, washed, stemmed and finely chopped
1 cup water
2 eggs, lightly beaten
¼ cup finely chopped scallions, including green tops

Wash the fish under cold water and pat the pieces completely dry with paper towels. Sprinkle the fish evenly on all sides with the tablespoon of salt. In a heavy 10-12 inch skillet, heat 1 cup of oil over moderate heat until it is hot but not smoking. Add all the fish, arranging the pieces in one layer. Fry for 5 or 6 minutes on each side or until each piece is crisp and richly browned. Remove the fish to a hot platter, discard the oil in the skillet. Wash and dry the skillet, and heat the remaining 2 tablespoons of oil until a light haze forms above it. Drop in the garlic and stir for a minute or so until it browns lightly. Then add the onions, stirring frequently, cook for about 5 minutes until they are soft and translucent but not brown. Watch carefully for any sign of burning and regulate the heat accordingly. Add the tomato and continue to cook for 3 or 4 minutes. Stir in the cup of water and teaspoon of salt and return the fish to the skillet. Pour in the eggs and stir them gently into the sauce until they form soft creamy curds. Sprinkle the top with the scallions and serve at once directly from the skillet.

12 TROUT AMANDINE

A restaurant favorite; here's how they do it:

> 4 trout fillets
> Flour and salt
> 1/2 cup butter
> 1/2 tsp. onion juice
> 1/4 cup blanched, finely slivered almonds
> 1 tablespoon lemon juice

Wash and dry the fish. Dust with salt and flour. Heat half the butter and onion juice in a heavy skillet and cook fish until lightly browned. Remove and place on a hot serving dish. Pour off the grease remaining in the pan and add the rest of the butter. Add the almonds and brown slowly, then add lemon juice and when it foams, pour it over the fish.

13 CHEESE-COATED PERCH

Save those larger perch and give them this treatment:

> 1 pound fresh perch fillets (or other freshwater fish)
> 1/4 cup all purpose flour
> 1 beaten egg
> 1 tsp. salt
> Dash pepper
> 1/4 cup fine dry bread crumbs
> 1/4 cup grated Parmesan cheese
> 1/4 cup shortening
> 1 eight ounce can tomato sauce
> 1/2 tsp. sugar
> 1/2 tsp. dried basil leaves, crushed

Cut fish into serving size portions. Coat with flour and dip into a mixture of egg, salt and pepper, then dip into a mixture of bread crumbs and cheese. Fry fish slowly in a skillet of hot shortening until browned on one side. Turn and brown other side. Combine tomato sauce, 1/4 cup water, sugar and basil in a saucepan. Simmer 10 minutes and serve with the fish.

14 PERCH WITH PARSLEY AND DILL

This is a turn-of-the-century favorite:

> 8 medium sized perch, dressed (scale and remove heads, tails, and fins; and drain.)

Cover bottom of baking dish with ¼ cup finely chopped parsley and arrange the fish in the baking dish.

Top with:

> 2 tablespoons finely chopped parsley
> 2 tablespoons chopped fresh dill or
> 1 tsp. dill seed

Pour ¼ cup hot water around the fish. Bake at 350° for 20 to 25 minutes and serve. Whole crappies and sunfish also respond well to this treatment.

15 POTATO FISH

You won't believe this until you try it.

> 4 fresh fillets (any fish including catfish & bullheads)
> 1 beaten egg
> 1 cup instant mashed potato flakes
> 1 envelope onion salad dressing mix
> Salad oil

Season fish with salt and pepper. Combine egg and 1 tablespoon water. Combine potato flakes and dressing mix. Dip fish into egg mixture, then roll in potato mixture. Repeat. Brown fish in hot salad oil on one side for 4 to 5 minutes. Turn carefully and brown second side. Drain on paper toweling.

16 SWEET AND SOUR FISH

This one's straight from China!

Ingredients:

> 1 fresh fish, bass, walleye, etc. about 3 pounds live weight, scaled and dressed.
> cornstarch
> 1½ quarts oil
> Sweet and sour sauce (below)

With a sharp knife make 5 or six *deep* diagonal slashed on each side of fish. Shake fish so that it opens up. Sprinkle both sides with cornstarch. Heat oil in a large iron kettle or pan to 375° and carefully place fish into oil. You can cut fish in half and fit together after cooking if your kettle is not large enough. Fry 7 to 10 minutes on each side, until deep golden brown turning gently. Carefully remove from kettle and drain well. Place on a large platter and serve with warm sweet and sour sauce.

Sweet and Sour Sauce:
¾ cup sugar
½ cup Chinese wine or cider vinegar
½ cup catsup
½ cup water
juice of 1 lemon
1 tsp. soy sauce
¼ cup cornstarch dissolved in ¼ cup water
¼ cup frozen baby peas

Combine sugar, vinegar, catsup, water and lemon juice in a saucepan. Cook over medium heat 3 to 4 minutes. Stir in soy sauce and dissolved cornstarch. Bring to a boil, stirring constantly. Cook until thick and clear. Stir in the peas and heat for 3 minutes and pour over fish.

17 PERCH TEMPURA

Ingredients:
2 lbs. fresh fish fillets, salted to taste
1 lemon, halved
½ Tempura Batter recipe
1 qt. vegetable oil

Cut fish fillets into bite-sized pieces and drain well on paper toweling. Season with salt and squeeze lemon juice over the fish.

TEMPURA BATTER

2 c. sifted flour
3 egg yolks
2 c. ice water

Sift the flour 3 times. Combine the egg yolks and water in a large bowl over ice and beat with a whisk until well blended. Add the flour gradually, stirring and turning the mixture from the bottom with a spoon. Do not overmix. The flour should be visible on top of the batter. Keep the batter over ice while dipping and frying.

Spear pieces of fish and dip in the batter, drain slightly and fry in deep fat heated to 360 degrees for about 5 minutes, turning to brown evenly.

18 FRYING PANFISH (sunfish and crappies)

Large sunfish and crappies may be filleted and prepared by any of the foregoing recipes; however, average size and smaller panfish are more easily fried whole.

Scale the fish; remove head, tail, and fins; and draw.

Season the fish inside and out with salt and pepper (use lemon-pepper if available).

Dip the whole fish in a batter of water and eggs (1 egg to 1 cup of water).

Roll the fish in cracker crumbs or corn meal or bread crumbs. (If you prefer flour, batter is not necessary.)

Fry on both sides in a generous portion of oil until brown. For larger fish, cover the pan after you turn the fish and add a few drops of water to steam-cook the fish. Then remove the cover and brown for a crisper skin.

If you prefer to fry your fish in butter, use low heat and cook considerably longer until it flakes easily. Do not let the butter burn.

19 WHOLE BABY WALLEYES

Don't despair when a little walleye is too injured to throw back. Scale it, remove head, fins, tail and entrails. Fry as you would a panfish.

20 WALLEYE FILLETS WITH SKIN ON

It is no coincidence that fish bought in the market have their scales removed and the skin on. Much of the walleye flavor is in the skin. Walleyes are difficult to scale; but it is worth the effort. Fry according to any of the recipes in this chapter, with the skin side especially crisp.

21 SMELT

These little silvery fish from the Great Lakes—that drive noramlly sane people apparently out of their minds as they drive hundreds of miles and stay up half the night are worth the effort, providing you eat them fresh. They are an oily fish and the flavor deteriorates rapidly. Keep them on (and in) crushed ice until you get home; then enjoy them immediately. They may be frozen in water and will still be good to eat, but not as delicious as fresh.

Smelt may be fried according to any of the recipes in this chapter but are probably at their best coated with beer batter and fried in deep fat.

Smelt may also be pickled or made into "sardines" according to the recipes on pages 59 and 77.

TIPS FOR CATCHING WALLEYE PIKE

- When walleyes are hungry they will bite on most anything, but at such times artificial baits may make a full stringer come more easily.
- When fishing is slow, live bait such as a minnow, leech, or worms are often more productive.
- Day in and day out it is very hard to beat a baited jig, tied directly to your monofilament line (no leader) and worked along the bottom. For some reason baited jigs without feathers (just the painted lead head) seem to be better than those with feathers. Use a minnow, part of a crawler, or leech. Jigs with feathers (especially maribou hair) can be very productive even without bait if jigged *vigorously*.
- When using a jig spoon (such as a Swedish pimple or Dr. Lund's Little Swede), jig it very hard without bait or work it in short, tantalizing twitches *with* bait (minnow, part of a crawler, or leech). When using a minnow, hook it through the nose when casting or trolling or under the back fin when fishing below the boat or through the ice.
- A bright moon improves night fishing for walleyes.
- Walleyes are bottom feeders, keep your bait within one foot of the bottom.
- In springtime, look for walleyes in relatively shallow water (6 to 8 feet), near spawning locations. In summer, try deeper water (12 to 30 feet or even more) but don't overlook such feeding spots as sandbars, reefs, or along weedbeds—especially early morning, at noon, or in the evening. In winter, look for walleyes in deeper holes in the daytime (over 15') or on sandbars or nearer shore early morning, in the evening, or after dark. For night fishing, try very shallow water (6 or 7 feet or even less). In the fall return to the spring haunts. Walleyes are usually found in schools.

- Jigging through the ice for walleyes with a small baited spoon can sometimes be more productive than live bait alone. Try baiting the spoon with a small minnow, or the front ⅓ of a dead minnow, or the eye of a walleye.
- When using live bait, give the walleyes time to take it. This will vary from time to time depending on how hungry the fish are. Leeches usually take only a few seconds; minnows take a little longer, and night crawlers may take as long as a minute. Use the whole crawler and a small hook (#6) imbedded in the head of the worm.
- When using a bobber (use the pencil variety or one that is balanced to just break the surface so that the walleye will not be able to detect any resistance) do not set the hook until the second run; this will indicate that the walleye has had time to ingest the bait.

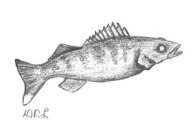

chapter III

BAKED DISHES

Larger fish often taste better from the oven than from the frying pan. Just as your mouth "waters" occassionally for a beef roast with "all the trimmings" instead of steak—you will find baked fish a great alternative to fried fillets.

22 MINNESOTA BAKED NORTHERN with RAISIN STUFFING

This recipe works equally well with muskies or whitefish. On the other hand, all fish are not good baked; even the tasty walleye or the flavorful bass are only fair unless they receive special treatment and seasonings.

Northerns or muskies should weigh five pounds or more, whitefish at least three.

Preparing the fish: Scale and gut the fish; remove the head, tail and all fins. Wash and dry the fish, inside and out.

Score the back of the fish with cross-section cuts about three inches apart—down to the backbone.

Salt and pepper, inside and out and in the cuts.

Preparing the stuffing

 1 cup raisins
 ¼ lb. butter (added to one cup hot water)
 2 cups croutons or dry bread crumbs
 1 large onion, chopped but not too fine.
 salt and pepper
 1 cup chopped bologna (or wieners or polish sausage or
     luncheon meat)

Place the croutons, raisins, meat, and onions in a bowl. Salt and pepper lightly while stirring the ingredients together.

Add and stir in the butter-hot water mixture just before stuffing the fish.

Lay a sheet of foil on the bottom of the roaster.

Stuff the fish (loosely) and place upright on the sheet of foil. Fold the foil up along both sides of the fish—do not cover the back. The foil will hold in the stuffing. If your fish is too long for the roaster, you may cut it in two and bake the two sections side by side.

Leftover stuffing or additional stuffing may be baked in a foil package alongside the fish or even outside the roaster.

Place a strip of bacon and a slice of onion, alternately, over each score (or cut).

Cover the roaster and place in a preheated, 300° oven. After one hour, remove cover and continue to bake until the meat becomes flaky and separates from the backbone (as viewed from the end of the fish). This should take about another half-hour, depending on the size of the fish.

Transfer the baked fish to a platter. Cut through the backbone at each score mark, separating the fish into serving-size portions. The stuffing may be lifted out with each portion as it is served.

Serve with tartar sauce and/or lemon.

23 LEMON-RUBBED and WINE-BASTED BAKED FISH WITH WILD RICE DRESSING

Choose a large northern pike, muskie or whitefish. Scale and draw the fish; remove the head, tail, and fins; wash thoroughly inside and out and dry.

Strain the juice of three lemons; salt lightly. Rub the inside and the outside of the fish—thoroughly—with the salted lemon juice. Refrigerate the fish for two or three hours.

Prepare stuffing:

1 cup wild rice, washed (will make three cups cooked rice)[1]
½ cup melted butter or margarine mixed with ½ cup hot water
1 large onion, chopped
⅓ pound chopped bologna or summer sausage or polish
    sausage or luncheon meat
1 cup celery, chopped
1 small green pepper (or ⅓ cup)

---

[1]You may substitute 1 cup raisins for the wild rice and add 1½ cups croutons. You could also use ½ white and ½ wild rice.

Cook the wild rice:
>3 cups of water
>1 cup wild rice (washed)
>salt and pepper
>¼ lb. melted butter or margarine

Season water with one tablespoon salt and bring to a boil. Add rice and lower the heat so that the water just simmers. Cook—covered—for about 45 minutes or until the kernels are well opened and the rice is tender. Do not overcook.

Pour off any water that has not been absorbed. Add pepper and a little more salt to taste; pour on the melted butter, and fluff with a fork.

Sauté the celery and onions:

Cook slowly in butter or margarine for about three minutes or until the onions are translucent and the celery is light brown.

Combine:

The wild rice, onion, celery, chopped meat, and green pepper. Season lightly with salt and pepper. Pour ½ cup melted butter combined with an equal amount of hot water over the mixture and stir the ingredients together—thoroughly.

Stuff and bake:

Pat the chilled fish dry and stuff loosely. Left over dressing may be baked separately in foil along side the fish. Place a sheet of foil in the bottom of a roaster, then place the fish in the roaster (back up). Bring the foil up half way around the fish to hold in the stuffing. Place in a pre-heated medium oven (350°).

Melt ¼ pound of butter and add an equal amount of white wine. Baste fish from time to time with the wine-butter mixture.

Bake until the meat flakes easily from the large end of the fish (about 15 to 20 minutes per pound).

Transfer baked fish to serving platter; garnish with parsley and serve with lemon wedges.

24 BAKED FILLETS

Select two pounds of walleye or other freshwater fish fillets.
Season with salt and pepper on both sides.
Dip in milk and coat both sides with bread crumbs.
Place on a well-greased cookie sheet or in a shallow baking dish.
Bake in a pre-heated medium oven (about 325°) for about 40 minutes.

Meanwhile, prepare a solution of:

   3 tablespoons lemon or lime juice
   3 tablespoons melted butter

Spoon most of the liquid over the fillets after the fish has been in the oven about 5 minutes. About ten minutes later (15 minutes baking time), sprinkle the remainder of the lemon-butter mixture over the fish and shake paprika and parsley flakes over the fillets. Remove and serve after a total of about 40 minutes baking time or when the fillets flake easily.

25 BAKED FILLETS AND DRESSING

Use walleye, northern, or other fairly large fillets.

Prepare your favorite stuffing or choose any one of those described in this cookbook such as the raisin or wild rice recipes just described.

Lay the fillets on a well-greased cookie sheet or in a shallow baking dish and smother with stuffing.

Bake in a moderate oven (325°) for about one hour. Turn on the broiler the last couple of minutes (but watch closely) to give the dressing a crusty brown coating.

26 LEMON STUFFED FISH

4 fish fillets (1½ pounds each)

Ingredients:

   ½ cup finely chopped celery
   ¼ cup chopped onion
   3 tablespoons butter
   4 cups dry bread cubes or croutons
   ½ tsp. grated lemon peel
   4 tsp. lemon juice
   1 tablespoon snipped parsley
   1 tablespoon butter, melted

Place 2 fillets in a greased baking pan. Cook celery and onion in 3 tablespoons butter until crisp tender. Pour over bread. Add lemon peel and juice, parsley, ½ tsp. salt and a dash of pepper, and toss together. Spoon half the stuffing mixture on each fillet in the pan.

Top with remaining two pieces of fish, brush with 1 tablespoon butter. Sprinkle with salt and paprika and bake, covered at 350 for about 25 minutes.

27 FRESH FISH STUFFED WITH SEAFOOD

Ingredients:
- 2 cups cooked chopped shrimp or crabmeat
- 3 to 4 pounds boned fillets
- 2 eggs
- 1 cup cream
- 2 tablespoons butter
- ½ cup chopped canned or fresh mushrooms
- 2 tsp. chopped chives
- 1 tablespoon flour
- Salt and paprika
- 4 tablespoons sherry
- 2 limes

Mix the shrimp, egg and ½ cup of the cream together. Melt butter, add mushrooms and chives and sauté until soft, add flour and cook. Add shrimp mixture and cook until thick. Place fish in a buttered baking dish and spread the mixture between the two sides of the fish. Pour over the remaining cream, sprinkle with salt and paprika. Add sherry (optional) and bake at 350° for 45 minutes. Serve with fresh lime quarters.

28 BAKED FISH WITH SOUR CREAM

Preheat oven to 350°

Ingredients:
- 4 lbs. of fish fillets
- 3 cups cultured sour cream

Rub fillets with paprika and butter. Place in an ovenproof dish and cover with the sour cream. Cover the dish and bake about 35 minutes, or until done.

Before serving, sprinkle with chopped parsley.

29 STUFFED ROLLED FILLETS

For two pounds of boneless walleye fillets (other varieties also work very well), prepare the following dressing:

Ingredients:
- 3 cups seasoned croutons
- 1 cup chopped celery
- ½ cup chopped onion
- ¼ pound butter or margarine
- ½ cup hot water

(You may add other of your favorite stuffing ingredients such as sliced almonds, raisins or mushrooms.)

Sauté the celery and onion in butter or margarine over low heat until the onions are translucent and the celery light brown. Add ½ cup hot water and pour the mixture over the croutons—mix well.

Pre-heat the oven to 325°
Lightly season the fillets on both sides with salt and pepper.
Spread the stuffing over the fillets in a thin layer.
Roll up the fillets and fix with toothpicks.
Place in a roaster or baking dish and cover.
Place in the pre-heated oven (325°) for 30 minutes.

While waiting for the fillets to bake, prepare a sauce from the following ingredients:
4 tablespoons lemon juice
6 tablespoons melted butter
4 tablespoons cooking sherry or white wine

When the fish in done, spoon the lemon-butter-wine sauce over the rolled-fish and serve.

30 SLOW-BAKED, STUFFED BASS

Use a four pound bass (or larger if you're a lucky fisherman). Either large or small mouth variety works well. Scale the fish, draw, and remove the head, tail, and fins. Rub fish inside and out with lemon juice or wedges. Season lightly—inside and out—with salt and pepper.

Prepare stuffing from the following ingredients: (for a larger fish, increase the ingredients proportionately.)
2 cups seasoned croutons
1 onion, chopped
¼ green pepper, chopped
1 cup celery, chopped
⅓ pound diced ham (Most any kind of ham luncheon meat will also work well)
¼ pound butter or margarine, melted
⅓ cup hot water

Sauté the onion and celery in butter over low heat until cooked (light brown).

Add the chopped ham, green pepper, and hot water. Pour the mixture over the croutons and mix well.

Pre-heat oven to 225°. (low heat)

Place a large sheet of foil (enough to wrap the entire fish) in the bottom of the roaster.

Place slices of onion and pieces of bacon alternately the length of the back of the fish.

Pull the foil up around the fish and seal.

Place in roaster (without cover) in slow oven (225°) and bake 3½ hours (up to an hour longer for fish larger than 4# dressed weight).

The last half hour, unfold the foil exposing the back of the fish and continue baking.

Transfer fish to serving platter with spatulas. If the fish breaks apart, re-shape. Garnish with parsley and serve with lemon wedges.

31 BAKED FILLETS ON MUSHROOMS

Step #1: Prepare the mushrooms.

For two pounds of fillets, (walleye or de-boned northerns are especially good) use about one pound of fresh mushrooms.

Chop mushrooms into bite-size pieces.
Melt 6 tablespoons of butter.
Sauté ¼ cup chopped onion in the butter (about three minutes)
Add the chopped mushrooms and continue to cook slowly for about 5 minutes.

Set the mushrooms aside until the fillets have been baked. (If fresh mushrooms are not available, you may use pre-cooked, canned mushrooms.)

Step # 2: Bake the fillets.

Lay the fillets in a shallow baking dish.

Add ½ cup water, ½ cup white wine, ten whole black peppers, and 1 bay leaf.

Bake in a medium oven (350°) for 30 minutes.

Step #3: Prepare a sauce.

Just before removing the fish from the oven, melt 3 tablespoons of butter or margarine. Stir in 3 tablespoons flour while the mixture cooks slowly (for a couple of minutes).

Pour the juices off the fillets into the butter-flour mixture—slowly stirring all the while.

When the sauce has thickened, remove from heat and stir in ⅔ cup cream. Season to taste with salt and pepper.

Step #4: Finally—

Cover the bottom of a second baking dish with the mushrooms,
Lay the fillets on this bed of mushrooms.
Cover the fillets with the cream sauce.

Return to a hot oven (450°) for a few minutes until lightly
    browned.
Garnish and serve.
Summary of ingredients:
    1# fresh mushrooms (or large can mushroom pieces)
    9 tablespoons butter
    ½ cup water
    ½ cup white wine
    10 peppercorns
    1 bay leaf
    3 tablespoons flour (all purpose)
    ⅔ cup cream
    Salt and pepper

32 FILLETS BAKED IN FOIL

Wash, dry and season the fillets.

Lay each fillet on a separate foil sheet.

On each fillet place a generous pat of margarine or butter, a thick slice of onion, and a ring of green pepper.

Fold the foil over the fillet and seal.

Place the package in a preheated 300° oven for twenty minutes. (Thick fillets take a little longer)

Serve with tartar sauce and/or lemon. You will enjoy a new taste experience that you will want to try again and again. You may also prepare fish in this manner for shore lunch—just bake them over coals.

33 BAKED IN THE CAMPFIRE

Clay is essential to this recipe, but it is probably available more places than you think. It is commonly found in the banks of most rivers and streams in the upper Midwest or in the lowlands near lakes. If you suspect the soil may contain clay, add a little water and try molding it with your hands.

Use whole, dressed fish rather than fillets. Scale and take off the head, tail, and fins. Since it is difficult to envelope a large fish in clay, select smaller walleyes or bass or try crappies or sunfish.

Season the inside of the body cavity with salt and pepper.

Wrap the fish tightly in foil to keep out all dirt.

Moisten the clay until it can be worked with your hands. Mold the clay entirely around the fish—at least ½ inch thick.

Place the fish in the coals of the fire for one hour.

Break the clay open; unwrap the foil; split the fish open down the backbone into the two halves.

Serve with potatoes, also roasted in the fire.

34 CHARCOAL BAKED WHOLE FISH

For a real out-door flavor, give this recipe a try.

Dress a large fish, such as a northern pike, muskie, whitefish, or lake trout. Walleye is not at its best baked, but this may well be the best of the baking recipes for this delicious fish. Scale the fish (unless it is a lake trout). Cut off the head, tail, and fins. When you draw the fish, make a single cut down the center of the stomach so that the body cavity will hold as much stuffing as possible.

Prepare your favorite dressing—or try this one:

    3 cups croutons or dry bread crumbs
    1 large onion, chopped
    1 cup celery, chopped
    1 small can mushrooms, sliced
    ¼ pound (1 stick) margarine or butter, melted
    ½ cup hot water

If croutons are not seasoned or if you use bread crumbs, season with salt and pepper and ½ teaspoon sage and/or poultry seasoning.

Sauté the onion in the butter or margarine; when the onion is translucent (but not brown), add the ½ cup hot water. Place the croutons (or bread crumbs) and chopped celery in a bowl. Pour the butter-water-onion mixture over the contents and stir well. Add seasoning—evenly.

Stuff the body cavity and sew up the fish. Extra dressing may be prepared by wrapping it in foil and placing it along side the fish on the grill.

Place the fish on its side on the charcoal grill (over pre-ignited charcoal that has turned gray, thus indicating it is ready). If your grill has a cover, baking should take about 8 minutes per pound. Without a cover it will take about twice as long and you must turn the fish when it is about half done. You may check doneness by using a fork to see if the meat will flake easily around the exposed backbone at the large end of the fish. Baste from time to time with melted butter.

To avoid flames burning the fish, place a piece of foil directly under the fish and bank the charcoal on each side of the foil.

35 BULLHEAD WITH TOMATO SAUCE

Ingredients:

    3 1 lb. bullheads or other fish, dressed.
    1 eight ounce can tomato sauce
    2 tablespoons salad oil
    1 teaspoon cheese-garlic salad dressing mix or italian salad
        dressing mix
    ½ tsp. salt
    Grated Parmesan cheese

Place fish in a greased shallow baking pan. Combine tomato sauce, salad oil, dressing mix and salt. Brush inside cavities with sauce, pour remaining sauce over and around fish. Sprinkle with Parmesan cheese. Bake at 350° for about 40 minutes until fish flakes easily. Bullheads are also excellent fried.

MICROWAVE BAKED FISH

Different brands of microwave ovens require different times and slightly different treatment. Check your own manual before using any of these recipes.

36 WHOLE TROUT (OR OTHER SMALL FISH)

Dress a one pound trout per person. (Leave on head and tail but gut and wash.) Rub inside and out with lemon wedge; season lightly with salt and pepper. Lay in baking dish and cover head and thinner part with foil (providing foil may be used in your microwave). Cover with plastic; vent a few places with a fork.

About six minutes will cook one trout; add about three minutes for each additional fish.

Garnish with parsley and serve with lemon wedges and/or tartar sauce.

37 BAKED NORTHERN (OR OTHER LARGE FISH) WITH OYSTER STUFFING

Oyster dressing:

    1 cup chopped (not too fine) oysters
    1 medium onion, chopped
    ½ cup celery, chopped
    2 cups seasoned croutons or bread pieces
    salt and pepper (using less if croutons are pre-seasoned)
    1 stick butter (¼ #) melted
    ¾ cup hot water

Sauté the chopped onion in the melted butter until translucent (about 3 or 4 minutes over low heat). Mix with other ingredients.

Scale northern and remove head, tail, and fins and draw. Wash throroughly and rub inside and out with lemon wedge. Season lightly.

Stuff northern and set upright on oven-proof dish.

Brush outside of northern with Kitchen Bouquet and melted butter (in that order).

Cover with plastic (vented) and cook in microwave oven for about 20 minutes (for a northern that weighs 5 or 6#'s before cleaning). If fish does not flake easily, return to oven, estimating time by degree of doneness.

If fish is not brown enough, brush again with Kitchen Bouquet.

Brush with lemon-butter sauce before serving. (¼# melted butter and 1 tablespoon lemon juice)

38 BAKED CROSS-SECTION STEAKS

Use either fillets or cross section steaks from larger fish.

Lay fillets in an oven-proof baking dish in a single layer. Brush with lemon-butter sauce.

Season lightly with salt and pepper.

Bake 1 pound of fillets about 8 or 9 minutes; longer for more fish.

Serve with lemon or drawn butter. Flake off bite size pieces of fish and dip them in the melted butter. Better than lobster!

TIPS FOR CATCHING NORTHERN PIKE

- Northern respond to action and often strike more out of anger or greed than hunger. The more action you give your lure the better.
- Look for northern in relatively shallow water along rushes or weedbeds (or over weeds) and on bars or reefs. In mid-summer, however, they may be found in much deeper water (10-25 feet).
- Northerns do not feed at night (unless there is a very bright moon). Their major feeding periods are mid-morning, noon, and early evening.
- Northerns rarely hit surface lures. Generally speaking, they are most apt to see and to be attracted to lures fished about half-way between the bottom and the surface. However, when they are in the deeper waters during mid-summer, try bottom fishing. Lures worked over weedbeds (but just under the surface) are often very productive.

- Large minnows (6 to 9 inches) are excellent bait for big northerns (suckers, chubs, and shiners — in that order). Dead smelt also work well, especially in a current. Try minnows still fishing with a bobber or troll them hooked through the nose with a large Lindy Rig. With either technique, give them ample time to take the bait — at least a full minute. Giant northerns are often found in spring near sucker spawning grounds or in the fall where crappies are schooling up.
- Spoons, bucktails, crank baits and large "plugs" are effective when trolled or retrieved rapidly and radically. When trolling, move at least two or three times as fast as for walleyes.
- White jigs with red and white feathers (preferrable maribou hair) work very well — plain or baited. Use at least a 20# monofilament leader or the northerns are apt to bite the lure off.
- When spearing northerns (legal in Minnesota at this writing), use a live decoy (large minnow about 9 or 10 inches long in a harness) and an artificial decoy at the same time. Jerk the artificial decoy (spoon or wooden minnow) *very hard* for about a minute and then let it set for a few minutes — twitching it occasionally.

chapter IV

POACHING AND BOILING

Poaching or boiling achieves an entirely different taste effect. You will especially enjoy this treatment if you like seafoods. Freshwater fish prepared according to some of the following recipes may be compared favorably to lobster or Alaskan king crab.

39 POACHED FISH[1]

Here is a very different and exciting way to prepare firm and oily fish such as lake trout or whitefish.

Fillet the fish, remove skin, and cut into serving-size pieces about six inches long. (The size doesn't really matter; you just want the pieces small enough to handle easily in the container you use for poaching.)

Fill a kettle about two-thirds full with *cold* water. Salt heavily (about one tablespoon per quart). Place the pieces of fish in the *cold* water.

Add two or three bay leaves or any other spices you prefer, such as whole black pepper or whole allspice. Add two tablespoons of vingegar—this helps kill house odors.

Bring to a boil—gradually. When the water has attained a "rolling boil," cut the heat back so that the water just simmers. Allow the kettle to simmer for fifteen minutes or until the fish can be flaked with a fork. Be careful not to overcook; this will make the fish tough.

Remove the poached fish and place on a platter; drain. Flake the fillets with a fork into fairly large pieces (bite-size). Season with salt and pepper and brush the surface of each piece with melted butter.

[1]Courtesy Edward Morey, Motley, Minnesota.

The fish is now ready for serving, or—you may try stirring the fish, seasoning, and butter together, or instead of brushing the butter on the fish, serve melted butter on the side in a custard bowl or small dish and let your guests dip the fish as you would dip lobster.

40 POACHING IN A FRYING PAN

This treatment is especially suitable for small, whole trout (all kinds) or grayling; however, larger fillets may also be prepared in this manner. It is also a simple and convenient method of preparing fish over an open campfire.

If you propose to use whole fish, the frying pan will of course have to be large enough to fit them in.

While the fish are being cleaned (Remove head, tail, and fins and draw trout; grayling must also be scaled.), pour enough water into the frying pan to cover the fish. Add a dash each of salt, pepper, and celery salt. A bay leaf is also helpful but optional. Slice an onion; break the slices into smaller pieces and place in the water. Bring to a boil (for 3 or 4 minutes), then reduce heat and submerge the whole fish in the liquid. Let simmer for about 10 or 12 minutes or until the meat can be easily flaked from around the exposed backbone at the large end of the fish.

Serve with lemon wedges.

Fillets from larger fish may be prepared in the same manner.

41 POACHING WITH WINE AND MUSHROOMS

This recipe may be used with most any freshwater fish, but is especially good with walleyes, boneless northern fillets (see page 9), or smallmouth bass.

Use a greased baking dish or oven pan - just large enough to accomodate - in a single layer - the amount of fish you wish to prepare.

Cover the bottom of the container with a layer of chopped mushrooms (pre-cooked or from the can).

Lay the fillets or small, whole dressed fish on the bed of mushrooms. Season lightly with salt and pepper. (If using whole fish, also season the inside of the body cavity.) For variety, you may want to try other seasons such as celery salt, parsley flakes, or onion salt. A few slices of onion would also add flavor.

Cover the fish with a solution of ⅔ water and ⅓ white wine.

Poach very slowly on top of the stove or cover dish or pan with foil (vented with a few holes to allow steam to escape), and place in a medium oven (325-350°).

Check after 15 minutes; if fish flakes easily, it is done.
Garnish and serve with lemon or tarter sauce, or melted butter.

42 WISCONSIN TROUT BOIL

This recipe comes from the shores of Lake Michigan where it is used with all kinds of trout - from "lakers" to "browns."

Prepare about one pound of trout fillets per person.

Vegetables are boiled along with the fish. Use whole potatoes (skins on), carrots, onions, or other "root" vegetables.

Use a 12 quart kettle or larger. Special "fish boil kettles" are available in many locations around the Great Lakes. These kettles contain removable baskets which hold the fish and also leave vented covers.

Ingredients to serve six:
   4# trout fillets
   6 large potatoes - skins on but washed
   6 medium, sweet onions - peeled
   2 cups salt

Pour 8 quarts of water into the kettle and add potatoes. Cover and bring to a *rolling* boil. Now add the onions and/or other vegetables and 1 cup of salt.

Allow the vegetables to cook for 20 minutes before adding trout.

Place the fish in a dish towel or cheesecloth (unless your kettle comes equipped with a basket). Lower the fish into the water until they are completely submerged but not touching the vegetables on the bottom of the kettle. When the water resumes a *rolling* boil, add the other cup of salt and cover the kettle. If the cover is not vented, leave an opening for the escaping steam.

It is important that you maintain a *rolling boil* at all times or the food will be too salty.

After 10 or 12 minutes, check the fish for flakiness and the vegetables for softness. When the fish flake easily and the potatoes are readily penetrated with a fork, your meal is done.

Serve with drawn butter flavored with lemon juice and garnished with parsley flakes.

43 MILK POACHED WITH WHITE SAUCE

Either fillets or whole, smaller fish (up to 4#) may be used.

Ingredients:
   two pounds fillets (lake trout, walleye, etc.) or 3 to 4 pounds of whole trout
   ¾ cup milk
   ¾ cup water

1 tablespoon lemon juice
1/2 teaspoon salt
1/2 teaspoon allspice
6 whole black peppers
1 bay leaf

Place the fish in a skillet. Add milk, water, lemon juice, and spices. (The liquid need not cover the fish.)

Cover and poach over low heat for twenty minutes. Do not scorch the milk.

Meanwhile, prepare a white sauce:

2 tablespoons butter
2 tablespoons flour
1 cup milk
a little salt and pepper
2 tablespoons lemon juice

Melt the butter - carefully, without burning - in a sauce pan or double boiler. Add the flour and continue to cook for three minutes, stirring continuously. Stir in the lemon juice.

Remove pan from the heat and slowly stir in the cup of milk.

Return the pan to the stove and bring to a boil, stirring all the while.

Place mixture in a double boiler, add salt and pepper, and cook until the sauce thickens.

Beat with an egg beater.

When fish flakes easily, remove to serving platter - using spatulas. Garnish with parsley and serve with white sauce.

44 NEW ENGLAND FISH BOIL

This differs from the "Wisconsin Trout Boil" recipe in that it calls for a whole fish - up to 15 pounds. This works well with any kind of larger trout or a medium size lake trout or salmon.

Select a kettle which will permit you to completely submerge the fish but without letting it touch bottom.

Draw the fish and remove head, tail, and fins.

Measure the water by the quart as you add it to the kettle until you have enough to cover the fish by several inches. For every 6 quarts of water add:

1/3 cup salt
1/3 cup lemon juice (vinegar may be substituted)
2 bay leaves
8 whole black peppers (peppercorns)
1 large, whole onion (peeled)

4 long pieces (stalks) celery - chopped
1 tablespoon allspice

Cover kettle and bring solution to a rolling boil for 10 minutes.

Submerge fish in dish towel or cheesecloth or lay on rack, taking care to keep fish off bottom of kettle.

After 12 or 15 minutes, check fish for flakiness at the large end - near the exposed backbone. If it flakes easily, the fish is ready.

Serve with lemon-butter sauce or a white sauce flavored with lemon (see Milk Poached recipe), or make this Hollandaise Sauce:

Ingredients:
¼ pound butter or margarine
1 tablespoon lemon juice
a couple of pinches of salt
2 egg yolks

Place half of the butter and all other ingredients in a double boiler. Stir until the butter is completely melted. Add balance of butter and stir until melted.

45 POACHED FISH (FILLETS) IN WINE SAUCE

To 2 lb. fresh fish fillets (any variety) add the following ingredients:
¼ cup sliced onion
2 sprigs parsley
4 celery leaves
1 cup dry white wine
¾ cup boiling water
1 tsp. salt

SAUCE
⅓ cup butter
3 tablespoons flour
1½ cups cooking liquid from fish
1½ tsp. salt
Dash Pepper
2 tsp. lemon juice
1 hard-cooked egg, sliced
¼ cup sliced toasted almonds

1. Arrange fish in a single layer in a large skillet with a tight-fitting lid.
2. Add onion, parsley, celery leaves, wine, boiling water and salt and bring to a boil.
3. Reduce heat, simmer covered 5 minutes or until fish flakes easily.
4. Carefully remove fish from skillet, arrange on a heated platter to keep warm. Strain cooking liquid, reserving 1½ cups.

5. Make sauce, in medium saucepan melt butter, remove from heat, stir in flour to make a smooth mixture.
6. Gradually stir in cooking liquid from fish, add salt and pepper, bring mixture to a boil, stirring.
7. Reduce heat, simmer 1 minute. Remove from heat. Stir in lemon juice, egg slices and almonds.
8. Spoon some of sauce over fish, pass the rest.

46 BOILED FRESHWATER HERRING

Remove heads, tails, fins, and entrails - one or two fish per person. The "true" Scandinavian leaves the heads on for "handles" when removing the backbones!

Place in boiling salted water (1 teaspoon per quart) for about 15 minutes or until the backbone can be pulled *easily* from the meat, leaving delicious flakes and morsels. Season to taste with salt and pepper. Pour melted butter over the fish and fluff with a fork.

Serve with boiled potatoes.

Herring may also be fried. Scale and clean the fish, season, roll in flour, and then fry crisp in fairly deep oil. But there will be a lot of bones.

Early Scandinavian settlers in the Midwest brought with them the custom of broiling herring over an open fire, holding them with tongs.

47 SMELT IN BARBECUE SAUCE

1 pound fresh smelt

Ingredients:
1 8 ounce can tomato sauce
½ cup chopped onion
2 tablespoons brown sugar
2 tablespoons vinegar
1 tablespoon Worcestershire sauce
1 tablespoon water
2 teaspoon prepared mustard
¼ tsp. salt

Clean, rinse and wipe smelt dry. Combine all ingredients, except smelt. Marinate smelt in tomato mixture, covered in refrigerate for several hours. In a large skillet bring smelt and tomato mixture to boiling. Reduce heat and simmer uncovered til fish are done. 8 to 10 minutes. Makes 3 to 4 servings.

TIPS FOR CATCHING LARGEMOUTH BASS

- Bass fishing is most fun with surface lures, but it is no sport for a man with a weak heart! One is never quite ready for the explosion that occurs when a largemouth breaks water with the "plug" in its mouth. Best action is very early morning or evening. Bass do bite at night but it is hard to spot cast in the dark. Casting accuracy is especially important with bass. Favorite haunts include weedbeds, rushes, stumps, lily pads, docks, or trees and bushes standing in flood waters.
- Surface lures - such as poppers or wounded minnows - should be twitched and "chugged" in a tantalizing fashion in contrast to the speed retrieve so effective with northern pike. As the bait hits the water, give it a little jerk, then let it set for 20 or 30 seconds before the next pull.
- Shallow running lures are often more productive than surface baits, but not as exciting at the moment of the strike. They have an advantage in that you need not wait for quiet water - so important to surface fishing. In addition to such old favorites as the Bass-oreno, the newer crank baits, and buzzer baits are very effective.
- Bass are not always in shallow water but may feed in depths of 10 feet or more, especially during the day. Plastic worms or live bait (minnows, nightcrawlers, or leeches) are especially effective in deeper waters.
- Bass often cruise through bull rushes and at such times may be taken with weedless lures such as buzzer baits and Shannon spinners.
- Frogs are an old reliable for bass and may be effectively fished on a hairless jig or with a large spinner or in a harness.

chapter V

BROIL AND FOIL

Broiled fillets are "just what the doctor ordered" for those on low fat diets.

Foil recipes are convenient, no fuss - no "muss," and always tasty.

48 BROILED FILLETS

A great alternative to frying - especially for those who are on grease-free diets. Any variety of fish may be prepared in this way, but whitefish, walleyes, and northerns are particularly tasty when broiled.

Wash and dry the fish; lightly season each fillet with salt and pepper.

Lay the fillets on a sheet of foil (to keep your oven clean).

Lay a piece of bacon on and under each fillet (cheap, fat bacon is best).

Place the fillets under the broiler for about ten minutes or less on each side. Be careful when you turn the fillets; they are very delicate. Place the bacon that was on the bottom on top of the fillet, and vice versa. The purpose of the bacon is to keep the fillets from drying out and from sticking to the foil. If you have no bacon on hand, baste with cooking oil, margarine, or whatever.

Serve with tartar sauce and/or lemon. It may remind you of lobster - but it is more tender. You may want to try dipping bite-size pieces into drawn butter (seasoned with a little salt and lemon).

49 WHOLE TROUT ON THE GRILL

Use a charcoal, gas or electric grill; broil in your oven; or grill over an open campfire.

Select fish 2# or less dressed weight - such as a small lake trout. Actually, any kind of trout will do or even a scale type freshwater fish such as a walleye - providing you remove the scales. Remove head, fins and tail and draw.

You will need plenty of heat but do not place the fish as close to the heat as you would a beef steak. You may like your steak burned on the outside and only warm and red in the middle - but fish must have time to cook all the way through without being burned too much on the surface.

Season the body cavity of the fish with salt and pepper.

Rub the skin thoroughly with cooking oil.

If you broil more than one fish, leave plenty of space inbetween for the heat to circulate. After about ten minutes, turn the fish over on the other side - using a spatula.

Allow another ten minutes and then check the end of the fish for flakiness - particularly around the exposed end of the backbone.

Remove carefully from the grill to a serving platter.

The skin will be burned and not edible, but the meat may be just about the best you've ever tasted!

50 PLANK-BROILED BY AN OPEN FIRE

If you are caught on a fishing trip without cooking utensils or if you just want to impress your family or friends with your knowledge of the out-of-doors or survival cooking - try this Indian method.

Start your campfire before you clean the fish so that you will have plenty of hot coals.

Although this method is more commonly used with trout, other freshwater varieties will do just fine. Two to six pounders have the most convenient size fillets. Fillet the fish but leave the skin on. If your fish has scales, remove them before filleting.

Select a clean board or hew a flat surface on a log.

Secure the fillets to the plank, flesh side out, preferably with wire or some other non-combustable material.

Season the flesh side with salt and pepper.

Prop the board as close as you can to the coals without the plank catching on fire - with the larger end of the fillet closer to the fire.

Brush the fish with butter or margarine from time to time during the broiling process.

Because the heat and the thickness of the fillet will vary, it is difficult to estimate the time needed to cook the fish - but when it is well browned, flake off a couple of small piece to test doneness.

The campfire will add a special flavor that will make the extra effort this method requires well worthwhile.

51 FOIL WRAPPED WHOLE FISH ON THE GRILL

Use heavy foil - lightly greased.

Select trout (any kind) up to 4# dressed weight. Walleye, northern, bass, crappie, or even large sunfish will also work just fine, but they first must be scaled. Remove head, tail, fins, and draw.

Rub the fish inside and out with lemon. Season lightly, but evenly, with salt and pepper.

Wrap the fish with foil (snugly) sealing the foil with an extra turn and pressing it between your fingers.

Place the fish on its side on the grill (charcoal, gas, electric, or over an open campfire). When using an open fire, position the fish over coals or low flames; do not allow the flame to lick the fish.

Roll the fish over on its side after 10 minutes. Smaller fish will take a little less time.

After another 10 minutes, open the foil at the larger end of the fish and check for flakiness. When the fish is done, it should flake away from the bones very easily.

For taste variations, wrap onion slices and/or green pepper rings in with the fish.

52 FOIL WRAPPED FILLETS

This technique provides an opportunity for a great variety of treatments - everything from a single fillet broiled in butter to a complete meal of fish and vegetables for several people, wrapped in a single package.

Use heavy duty foil - lightly greased.

Individual fillets may be wrapped in foil with a little butter (1/4 stick) and lightly seasoned with salt and pepper. Other seasonings may be substituted or added such as slices of onion, pepper, tomato, or combinations thereof. Broil the fillet about 7 or 8 minutes on each side. Actual time will vary with the thickness of the fillet.

A complete meal may be prepared for four in a single package:
   4# fillets (most any kind)
   6 medium, cooked potatoes - sliced (or two #2 cans)
   1 large onion, thickly sliced
   1 small green pepper, sliced

¼ pound butter (1 stick)
1 #2 can tomatoes (pour off juice)
Salt and pepper

Lightly grease a large piece of heavy duty foil and lay it flat.

Lay two pounds of fillets in the center of the foil; they may overlap slightly. Season lightly with salt and pepper.

Cover the fish with the sliced potatoes, onion, green pepper and tomatoes (without the juice).

Place the remaining two pounds of fillets on top of the vegetables and season lightly.

Bring the foil up over the meal and *seal well* all the way around.

Place on the grill for about 20-25 minutes, turning once.

Serve with hot coffee, bread, and a "doctored" can of baked beans. (Add brown sugar, catsup, and a little onion to the beans, stir, and heat. The amount of brown sugar and catsup will depend on your taste, but try 1/3 cup brown sugar and 1/3 cup catsup for a starter.)

53 CHARCOAL BROILED STEAKS

There is no special advantage to this technique unless you have a covered charcoal broiler - which seems to make the fillets much more flavorful.

Make an aluminum tray of heavy duty foil - double thickness.

When the charcoal is ready (gray), place the tray (well greased) on the grill and lay the fillets (single later) in the tray. Brush with melted butter or margarine and season with salt and lemon-pepper.

Cover the broiler and let cook for 10 minutes or until the fish flakes easily.

Garnish with parsley and paprika and serve.

54 PERCH AND PINEAPPLE

Here's a Hawaiian treatment for Midwest fish:

1 pound perch fillets (or other freshwater fish)
½ cup pineapple juice
1 tablespoon lime juice
2 tsp. Worcestershire sauce
½ tsp. salt

Cut fish into serving size portions. Place in a shallow baking dish. Combine pineapple juice, lime juice, worcestershire sauce, salt and a dash of pepper. Pour over fish marinate for 1 hour, turning once.

Drain, reserving marinade. Place fillets on a greased rack of a broiler pan. Broil 4 inches from heat until fish flakes. Brush occasionally with marinade. Heat remaining marinade and spoon over fish before serving.

SMALLMOUTH BASS

- The smallmouth is as different from the largemouth in its habitat and feeding as the walleye is from the northern pike. The smallmouth bass is more apt to be found in "walleye water." It inhabits bars, reefs, drop offs, points, and does well in rivers and streams. Use a "fish locator" or electronic depth finder to learn the structure of the water you are fishing.
- Although the smallmouth will occasionally hit a surface lure it is primarily a bottom feeder.
- Jigs (baited with a minnow, part of a crawler, or leech), spinner lures, Little Swede spoons, buzzer baits, artificial worms, and small "plugs" are all excellent.
- Smallmouths will take minnows but are more tempted by night crawlers and leeches worked along a reef or bar. Bobber fishing can be very effective if you know the depth so that the bait is kept fairly close to the bottom. Sometimes a crawler with the hook buried in the head and weighted down with only a split shot and allowed to squirm on the bottom or on a flat rock can be devastating.
- Crawfish are a favorite but only when the shells are soft.
- Smallmouths like a rocky bottom - perferrably stones about the size of an egg.
- In early June, during and just after spawning, bass fishing can be fantastic in shallow water (3 to 4 feet). Try bays or bars with gravel bottoms or very small stones.

chapter VI

GROUND, CHOPPED AND FLAKED

Here are some simple and effective ways of getting rid of the bone problem some varieties of fish present - such as the northern pike. Any fish may be used but it makes more sense to save such bone-free fillets as the walleye pike for some other treatment.

Fish hamburger is made by running the fillets through a meat grinder. Even an old fashioned, hand grinder will get the job done, but you may have to run the fillets through twice.

Those recipes which call for "chopped fish" refer to pieces about ¼" in diameter or about the size of chopped onion.

"Flaking" refers to picking the meat off the bones or separating the meat into its natural flakes with a fork - after the fish has been cooked.

55 GROUND NORTHERN

A real taste delight for fish lovers: a crisp-fried, hamburger size fish patty served on a bun and garnished with tartar sauce, lettuce leaf, and a slice of tomato.

If some bones sneak through, put the fillets through the grinder a second time.

Mix one egg into each pound of ground fish so that the patties may be formed more easily and will hold together better.

Fry the patties on both sides until brown - on a well-greased griddle or in a frying pan. If you like the outside of your fish-burgers crisp, try deep-fat frying; use enough oil so that the patty is about half-covered; when one side is done, turn the patty over. Be sure the oil is hot before you fry fish patties or they will absorb grease.

Leftover ground fish may be preserved by freezing.

56 FISH BALLS

Mix 1 cup bread crumbs with 1# ground northern.

Form into balls about 1 inch in diameter. Season the balls with salt and pepper (this may be done before they are formed, but be sure the meat is evenly seasoned).

Prepare a white sauce: (for one pound fish balls)

   4 tablespoons butter
   4 tablespoons flour
   2 cups milk
   a little salt and pepper

Melt the butter - carefully, without burning - in a sauce pan or double broiler. Add the flour and continue to cook for three minutes, stirring continuously.

Remove pan from the heat and slowly stir in the cup of milk.

Return the pan to the stove and bring to a boil, stirring all the while.

Place mixture in a double boiler, add salt and pepper, and cook until the sauce thickens.

Beat with an egg beater.

Place the fish balls in a casserole, covering them completely with the white sauce.

Place casserole in a preheated, 300° oven and allow to simmer for 1½ hrs.

Serve with boiled or mashed potatoes. Encourage guests to use additional seasoning - especially pepper.

57 FISH PATTIES[1]

Five pounds of fish fillets - diced (boneless). Walleye is probably the best but the recipe also works well with bass, northerns, crappies, etc.

   2 eggs
   1 cup pancake flour or bisquick
   ½ medium onion, chopped very fine
   ¼ medium green pepper, chopped fine
   ¾ cup milk

Dice the fish into pieces between ¼ inch "square."

Beat the eggs, then stir them together with the other ingredients in a bowl. The mixture should have the consistency of potato salad. If it is too "runny," add flour; it it is too stiff, add milk.

[1]Courtesy Neil Krough, Staples, Minnesota.

Preheat the griddle or frying pan at 325°. Coat liberally with peanut oil (or other cooking oil) and a large pat of margarine (to help in the browning process).

Spoon the mixture onto the griddle into patties about 3" in diameter and no more than one-half inch thick. Fry on both sides until golden brown. Serve with beans and fried potatoes.

These patties are really a special treat and they may even be enjoyed cold.

58 FISH PATTIES #2

Chop two cups of flaked boneless fish. Use most any fish which has already been cooked (trout, walleyes, northern, bass, etc.). This is a very good way of using left-overs. Combine the chopped fish with:

>2 eggs
>¼ cup chopped onion
>¼ cup water
>pinch of salt

Add cracker crumbs or bread crumbs until mixture has a consistency which can be easily molded into patties.

Fry on well-greased griddle or in a heavy frying pan until well-browned on both sides.

59 DEEP FAT FRIED FISH AND POTATO BALLS

This recipe is from the Deep South and probably was developed to make less desirable fish more palitable, but you may use any freshwater variety. However, if there are certain fish you like less than others, give them a try with this recipe.

Ingredients for 4 servings:

>1# boneless fillets
>5 large potatoes
>2 eggs
>½ cup milk
>2 tablespoons finely chopped onion
>salt and pepper

Peel the potatoes and quarter them.

Place the potatoes and the fish in a kettle and cover with cold water.

Bring to a boil and cook until the potatoes are done (easily penetrated with a fork). Skim from time to time if necessary.

Drain and then mash the potatoes and fish together - thoroughly.

Add the eggs to the milk and mix thoroughly. Add this mixture to the fish and potatoes and again mix thoroughly.

Season to taste.

Form into small balls - no more than 1 inch in diameter.

Meanwhile, pre-heat cooking oil to about 400°.

Deep fry the balls until a golden brown.

60 FISH CAKES

Ingredients for 4 servings:

    1# boneless fillets
    5 large potatoes
    2 eggs
    ½ cup water
    2 tablespoons chopped onion.
    salt and pepper

Peel and quarter the potatoes. Place them - and the fish - in a kettle and cover with cold water.

Boil until the potatoes are done. Drain and mash the fish and potatoes together - thoroughly.

Beat the eggs into the ½ cup of water. Add this to the fish and potatoes and mix again.

Form into patties (about the size of small hamburgers) - season, and fry on a well-greased griddle until brown on both sides.

Meanwhile, prepare a Hollandaise Sauce (see page 43) to serve over the cakes.

61 FLAKED TROUT SANDWICH SPREAD

Poach lake trout (or salmon) until the fish can be easily separated into flakes with a fork.

Mix two parts of flaked fish to one part of mayonnaise (or according to personal preference) and spread on sandwich bread.

Flakes from leftover fried fillets may also be used.

For variety - add finely chopped lettuce, celery, and/or green pepper (about ¼ cup each to each cup of flaked fish). Also - try substituting French dressing for part or all of the mayonnaise.

62 FLAKED TROUT CASSEROLE

Poach 1# of lake trout fillet until the fish can be easily flaked with a fork.

Ingredients to serve 4:

    Flaked trout from 1# fillet (a little over 1 cup)
    1 can mushroom soup
    1 3 oz. pkg. cream cheese

1 tablespoon chopped onion
1 tablespoon table mustard
¼ cup milk
2 tablespoons pimiento
1 cup cooked macaroni
½ cup bread crumbs
2 tablespoons melted butter

Soften the cheese and blend into the soup - using a blender or mixer. Stir in the flaked trout, onion, mustard, macaroni, milk, and pimiento.

Pour mixture into a casserole. Mix crumbs and melted butter and sprinkle on top.

Bake in medium oven (350°) for 25 minutes.

63 KEDGEREE

Flake northern, walleye, or salmon (use left-overs or poach). To 2 cups flaked fish add:

2 cups cooked rice
2 eggs, boiled and chopped
1 stick butter, melted (¼#)
salt and pepper (to taste)

Mix and fluff gently with fork; garnish with parsley.
Serves four.

TIPS ON CATCHING MUSKIES

- Muskie fishing is almost a disease. Once a fisherman has hooked or even seen the huge shadow of a lunker following his bait - he's addicted for life!
- Muskie feeding habits are similar to those of northerns but with some significant differences: muskies are more likely to hit a surface lure; they will feed later in the evening or even at night; and they seem to be more intelligent and therefore harder to deceive.
- Although muskie fishing is associated with over-size lures, many are caught on such small baits as jigs.
- Bait *action* is most important. When casting, use surface baits, jerk baits, spoons, or large crank baits and retrieve with speed and exaggerated, erratic motion. When trolling, travel at speeds about three times the rate you move for walleyes. However, it is important to vary the trolling speed; muskies often hit while you are accelerating. Large spoons (like Dr. Lund's Big Swede) and bucktails are good baits for trolling - as well as over-size plugs (such as the largest Rapala or Cisco Kid) and spinner lures.
- Muskies are found in and along weed beds, at the mouths of streams, along shorelines, and near or around logs, docks and other underwater structures. Most casting is done into relatively shallow water (3 to 6 feet) or over weedbeds; trolling is more effective on the deepside of weeds or rushes or along structure (6 to 12 feet).
- Spring and fall are the best times for taking the real lunkers, but hot, humid, summer days may also be very productive.

chapter VII

PICKLED FISH

Who doesn't like pickled herring? But why settle for second best? Freshwater fish are at least their equal. Northern pike and sunfish "pickle" especially well but experiment with other varieties - like crappies, tullibee, or smelt. But if you're still really hooked on herring, give Lake Superior freshwater herring a try!

64 PICKLED NORTHERN[1]

Fillet the fish as you would a walleye - don't worry about the bones. Cut fish into small (herring-size) pieces. Wash.

Prepare a brine solution by adding one cup of salt (preferably pickling salt) to four cups of water.

Cover the fish pieces with the brine solution and let stand overnight.

Step #2: wash off the pieces of fish and soak in white vinegar three to four days.

Step #3: drain, rinse, and place in jars (pint size is most convenient).

Prepare a pickling solution as follows:

To two cups of vinegar (if you like to use wine in cooking, use one cup of wine and one cup of vinegar) add -

one chopped onion (not fine)
one sliced lemon
2 tablespoons mustard seed (level)
1¾ cup sugar
4 bay leaves

[1]Courtesy Mrs. Donald Hester, Cass Lake, Minnesota.

5 whole cloves
1 tablespoon peppercorns (level)
5 or 6 small red peppers
1 tablespoon whole allspice

Bring the solution to a boil, then cool and pour over the fish.

Step #4: pour the pickling solution over the fish pieces you have already packed in the jars (fairly tightly). Cover and refrigerate at least three to four days before serving.

Five to six pounds of cleaned and cut-up northerns will yield approximately one gallon of pickled fish.

65 PICKLED FISH #2

Cut 5# of fish into "herring size" cubes. Cover with cold water. Stir in 1 cup of pickling salt and refrigerate for 2 days.

After 24 hours, wash the fish pieces thoroughly and drain on paper towel.

In a stone crock or large jar, place the fish, 1½ cups sugar, the thin slices of three large onions, 4 tablespoons pickling spices, and 2 bay leaves.

Cover with white vinegar and gently stir the ingredients together. Refrigerate for another 2 days.

Fish is now ready to eat and may be divided into smaller jars, but try to give each jar a fair share of onions and spices and be sure the fish are covered with white vinegar.

66 CEVICHE[1]

50-70 pieces or 3-6 lbs. of Salmon, Trout, Walleye or any oily fish, or mix. Cut fish in strips ½" wide x 1" to 2" long.

1 Pint of White Vinegar
2 Bottles (8 oz. each) Lime Juice (Real in bottle)
2 Medium Size Onions, sliced thinly
6 Bay Leaves
1 Diced Tomato (if you have it)
Whole Peppercorns (30 kernels)
½ Tsp. Ground Red Pepper
Few Whole Little Red Peppers (small hot chillies French's call them)
Tabasco - dash or so
Plenty of Salt

[1]Courtesy Mrs. George Cook, Hackensack, Minnesota.

Dry Mustard, a pinch
Parsley Flakes, a pinch
2 Tbsps. Olive Oil
Regular Pepper

Put all in glass or crockery bowl. Stir twice daily. You may have to add more salt after it stands awhile. You can tell by taste. Ready to eat after 24 hours. Keeps in refrigerator for week. If you wish you can add more fish to mixture when fish gets low. Put in refrigerator and stir once in awhile so fish all gets under the liquid.

TIPS ON CATCHING LAKE TROUT

- One of the real trophies of the fishing world, lake trout present a special challenge - even in the virgin waters of the far north.
- In early spring when the water temperatures are less than 50°F., the lazy man can fish in total relaxation from shore by "still fishing" with a smelt or a 3 to 4 inch square of scaled sucker meat on the bottom in from 20 to 40 feet of water. If suckers are not readily available - use large, dead sucker minnows from the bait shop. Mash them a little with your boot so that they are "nice and juicy." Sew the meat on the hook by weaving it into the sucker. With smelt or whole minnows, work a long shanked hook in the mouth, out the gill, and then bury the point under the back fin or as far back as the hook will go.
- In spring, while the trout are still feeding in relatively shallow water (20 to 40 feet), troll with large spoons (like Dr. Lund's Big Swede, of course!) or baited, hairless jigs (medium size fathead or sucker minnow). Using a fish locator or electronic depth finder, follow the structure around points and across bays - varying the depth between 20 and 40 feet. If you catch a trout at, say, 25 feet - troll at that depth for awhile.
- For really big lunkers, try speed trolling with muskie size baits. Vary the speed frequently; the trout will usually hit while you are accelerating.
- As the waters warm up, the trout will retreat to depths of 75 to 100 feet and more (except in the extremely far north - such as in the Northwest Territory). Trout may be caught at their summer depths by using lead core line, or a planning rig, or by jigging below a still or drifting boat. When jigging, drop the bait (jig with minnow) to the bottom or for about 100 feet, then retrieve it by reeling up rapidly for about six feet and then jigging for several minutes at that depth before reeling up another six feet. Continue reeling and jigging until you are within about 40 feet of the surface. A fish locator will help you find the depth at which the trout are feeding.

chapter VIII

GREAT LAKES SALMON

With the introduction of five varieties of salmon into the Great Lakes (Coho or Silver, Pink or Humpback, Atlantic, Chinook or King, and Sockeye), Midwest fishermen have an entirely new culinary challenge. The following are "tried and true" recipes from both coasts - including Alaska.

67 FRIED FILLETS

The "Fried Alaska" recipe on page 18, originated as a salmon recipe. There is no better way to fry salmon. Of course, fillets may be fried by the methods so traditional with freshwater fish, such as dipping them in egg and water and rolling them in cracker crumbs, corn meal or bread crumbs and then frying them on a well greased grill. They may be rolled in flour. Deep fat frying with your favorite batter (see pages 17 and 18) is also a good treatment. If the fillets are too thick for good frying, try slicing them in two - horizontally.

68 CROSS SECTION STEAKS

Here is a good treatment for those lunkers with fillets too thick to fry easily: Slice the dressed salmon into cross sections about ¾" thick.

Season lightly with salt and pepper.

Coat both sides with flour.

Fry slowly in butter.

Serve with lemon or tartar sauce.

69 BAKED SALMON

Dress the fish (remove the head, tail, fins and entrails).

Rub the fish, inside and out, with lemon wedges. Let chill in refrigerator up to four hours before baking.

Meanwhile, prepare your favorite stuffing or try this recipe:
Ingredients:

½ cup wild rice
1 medium onion, chopped
¾ cup celery, chopped
2 cups croutons
¼ cup shopped luncheon meat, or ham, or bologna
½ cup hot water (unless you prefer dry stuffing)
1 small can mushroom pieces
salt and pepper to taste. You may add a little sage if that is your preference.

Simmer the ½ cup wild rice in a cup and one-half of water for about forty minutes or until the kernels open. Rinse, drain, and fluff with a fork.

Sauté 1 medium onion (chopped) and ¾ cup celery (chopped) in ¼ # butter. This takes only 3 or 4 minutes over low heat. Add ½ cup hot water.

Pour the onion-celery-butter-water mixture over the croutons, chopped meat, and mushrooms (in a bowl). Stir thoroughly, seasoning to taste as you blend the ingredients.

Stuff the fish and sew up - or use foil under the fish in the roaster to hold in the dressing. Leftover stuffing may be baked in foil alongside the fish.

Bake, covered, in a medium oven (350°) for 15 to 20 minutes per pound or until the meat flakes very easily from around the backbone. For a more crispy skin, remove the cover the last 30 minutes. Sliced onions and/or bacon baked on top of the fish will also add flavor. A small cut across the back of the fish under each piece of bacon or onion will allow the flavor to penetrate more readily.

70 SALMON BOIL

Select and dress a medium size salmon (any variety).
Prepare a broth from these ingredients:

5 quarts water (use enough to cover the whole fish easily. Adjust the following seasoning accordingly (more or less) with the amount of water.
2 medium onions, sliced

½ cup lemon juice (vinegar may be substituted)
2 cups celery, chopped
4 tablespoons salt
10 whole black peppers (peppercorns)
2 bay leaves
2 spoons allspice

Bring to a boil, reduce heat and let simmer for 15-20 minutes.

Place the dressed salmon in cheesecloth or a dish towel and suspend in the kettle above the bottom, but make sure the fish is completely submerged. Bring to a boil, then again reduce heat and let simmer until the fish may be flaked easily from the bones (about 8-10 minutes per pound).

Serve with lemon wedges or Hollandaise Sauce (page 43)

71 BROILED SALMON

Traditionally, the entire salmon fillet (skin left on) is broiled on a plank along side an open campfire, basting it occasionally with butter. Similar flavor may be obtained more easily, however, by cutting the fish into cross-section steaks about ¾ inch thick and broiling them in your oven or over a gas, electric, or charcoal grill.

Season the steaks lightly with salt and pepper on both sides. Broil about seven minutes on each side.

Baste the second side with lemon butter a couple of times. (1 tablespoon lemon juice in ¼ pound melted butter)

Serve with lemon wedges.

72 SALMON BISQUE

1 cup flaked salmon (after poaching, or you may flake the fish from left-over baked or fried salmon.)
2 cans cream of celery or cream of mushroom soup
2 cans milk (if this is too creamy for your taste, use some or all water)
1 can consommé and 1 can water or 2 cups bullion (see page 77)
½ cup chopped onion
½ stick (1/8#) melted butter.

Sauté the onion in the melted butter for 3 or 4 minutes. Add to all other ingredients. Bring to a boil, then reduce heat and simmer for 15-20 minutes.

Garnish each serving with parsley flakes.

73 SALMON LOAF

Ingredients:

    2 cups flaked salmon (from left-overs or after boiling)
    2 cups bread crumbs
    salt to taste
    1 stick melted butter (¼#)

Mix salmon flakes, bread crumbs, and melted butter. Salt lightly as you mix.

Spoon into greased casserole or baking dish - about 2 inches deep. Bake in a medium oven (350°) for about 30 minutes.

Serve four.

74 SALMON SALAD

Service for 6
Ingredients:

    2 cups flaked salmon
    1 pkg. lemon or lime gelatin
    1 cup hot water
    ½ cup cold water
    ½ cup mayonnaise
    2 tablespoons vinegar
    1 cup celery, chopped
    ¼ cup onion, chopped very fine
    ¼ cup chopped parsley or lettuce
    pinch of salt

Dissolve the gelatin in 1 cup hot water - add cold water, vinegar, mayonnaise, and salt. Beat thoroughly, then refrigerate until partially set. Beat again until fluffy. Stir in salmon, celery, parsley or lettuce, and onion.

Pour into loaf pan and refrigerate until firm.

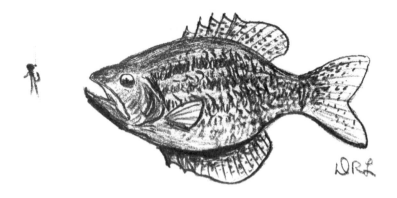

TIPS ON CATCHING CRAPPIES

- Crappies are very much a school fish - so it is usually "feast or famine" for the fisherman. Slow trolling is a good way to locate them.
- At "ice-out," crappies may be found for a few days in very shallow bays. As the lake begins to warm up, they will retreat to deeper water. Summer crappies may be located in and around weedbeds or near bull rushes providing the water is 6 feet deep or more. Fall and winter crappies seek deeper water, sometimes as much as 30 or 40 feet down.
- Crappies have a relatively small mouth; use small minnows or small jigs baited with tiny minnows.
- Crappie mouths are tender; carry a landing net for the big "slabs."
- Crappies usually bite with a delicate touch. If a bobber is used, be sure it is the "pencil" type or small enough that it will respond to the slighest action. Watch your bobber very closely for even the slightest movement (particularly in the wintertime).
- A fly rod can be a lot of fun when crappies are feeding on or near the surface. Feathered popper bugs work well.
- Crappies are often in the weeds but will sometimes feed just above them. They can be effectively fished at these times with a fly rod or with a spinning rod, bobber, and live bait - with only about a foot and one-half of line between the bobber and the minnow.
- Crappies will feed most anytime of the day or night.

chapter IX

GETTING MORE OUT OF YOUR CATCH — A BREAK WITH TRADITION

There is much more that can be done with a fish than the traditional frying, baking or broiling, and there are so called "rough" fish that can be absolutely delicious with the proper treatment. This chapter is devoted to a "break with tradition."

75 EELPOUT HORS D'OEUVRES (mock scallops)

Eelpout (freshwater cousins of the codfish) are actually very good filleted and fried. But because the meat is firmer than walleyes and northerns, they lend themselves very well to this recipe and will remind you of scallops.

Cut the eelpout fillets into bite-size pieces - about the size of scallops.

Season with salt and pepper.

Dip in water-egg batter (1 egg to a cup of water).

Roll in cracker crumbs.

Fry in about ¼ inch oil, turning until brown on all sides. The crisper the better - but not burned. Serve hot.

Now if you can forget what the fish looks like, get ready to enjoy a real delicacy! If you cannot forget, try walleye or perch tidbits.

Furthermore, there is nothing wrong with eelpout fillets - but don't hide the delicate flavor with heavy batter. People who have not had a look at this poor, ugly creature will choose eelpout over walleye nine times out of ten! Just tell them it's freshwater codfish.

76 NORTHERN PIKE INTO SALMON[1]

Impossible? Try it and see!

This recipe will dissolve the bones or soften them to the point where they will not be a problem. More important, the salmon-looking fish can then be used in any recipe calling for salmon or tuna fish (especially salads, casseroles, and sandwich spreads) or may be served cold as hors d' oeuvres.

For one pint:

2 cups of cut-up northern (bite-size) or other fish - even sucker
1 tablespoon cooking oil
1 tablespoon vinegar
1 tablespoon catsup
½ tablespoon salt

Combine all of the above ingredients and place in a pint jar.
Process in pressure cooker at 10 lbs. pressure for 90 minutes.

77 SMELT INTO SARDINES[1]

The smelters biggest problem is bringing home more smelt than he can really use or even give away. Right? Well, here's a great way to use and preserve these little fish - providing you like sardines.

2 tablespoons cooking oil
3 tablespoons vinegar
1 tablespoon salt (rounded)
1 pint smelt - cleaned

Prepare in a pressure cooker at 10 lb. pressure for 80 minutes.
Incidentally, smelt aren't bad pickled either.

78 WALLEYE CHEEKS

The cheek meat of a hog is a real delicacy; on the market it is labeled a "pork cutlet." Likewise with the "hogger" walleyes or lakers - save those cheeks; they, too, are a great delicacy when fried along with the fillets. You will find them a little more firm - like scallops.

79 SUNFISH AND CRAPPIE EGGS

In winter or early spring, save those panfish eggs! Just use the same batter as for the fish - and fry them. You have never tasted anything like it.

[1]Courtesy Mrs. Jerry Hayenga, St. Cloud, Minnesota.

80 NORTHERN PIKE LIVER

Another hors d' oeuvres treat. The liver of a good size northern or muskie can weigh a quarter pound. Cut into thin slices, season very lightly with salt and pepper, and fry over low heat - preferably in bacon grease. What will it taste like? Liver, of course!

81 SCANDINAVIAN FISH SOUP

1½ pounds boneless fish (salmon, walleye, northern, bass, trout, etc.), cut into half-inch cubes.
2 cups milk
3 cups water
½ cup celery, chopped
1 medium onion, sliced (pick apart the slices)
3 large potatoes, diced (bite-size chunks)
10 peppercorns
½ tablespoon salt
½ stick butter (1/8 pound)
1 tablespoon flour

Start with the 3 cups of water in a kettle; add the potatoes and bring to a boil. Add the fish, salt, whole black peppers, onion and celery and continue at a slow boil until potatoes can be easily pierced with a fork.

Mix the tablespoon of flour into the milk until smooth. Reduce heat to "simmer." Add the flour-milk mixture to the soup and stir until thoroughly blended. Add butter and continue heat until butter is melted (about 5 minutes).

82 FISH CHOWDER

Here's a great way to use your left-over fish or stretch that one fish you caught into a meal for the family.

½ cup chopped onion
¼ cup chopped green pepper
2 tablespoons butter
1 10 ¾ ounce can condensed tomato soup
1 14½ ounce can evaporated milk
1 chicken bouillon cube, crushed
Dash garlic powder
1 pound fresh fish cooked, poached and flaked (2 cups) - try bass, northern, or walleye.

In a 3 quart saucepan cook onion and green pepper in butter until tender but not brown. Add soup, evaporated milk, bouillon cube and garlic powder. Stir in the cooked fish and heat through.

83 FISH GUMBO

Here's another "fish-stretcher." This one from the Deep South. You will need the following ingredients:

¼ cup butter
½ cup chopped onion
1 medium-sized green pepper, chopped
½ cup chopped celery
1 28 oz. can of tomatoes
1 15½ oz. can okra
1 cup water
¼ tsp. dried thyme leaves
1 teaspoon salt
1 lb. fish fillets, cut into bite sized pieces
2 cups cooked rice

Melt butter in a large saucepan over moderately low heat. Add onion, green pepper and celery. Cook until tender (about 3 or 4 minutes). Add tomatoes, okra, water, thyme and salt and simmer for 15 minutes, stirring occasionally. Add fish and cook 10 minutes or until fish is easily flaked. Spoon ½ cup hot rice into each soup bowl before filling with the fish mixture.

84 FISH SPREAD AND DIP

Ingredients:

1½ cup cooked and flaked fish
1 cup dairy sour cream
1 envelope green onion dip mix
1 teaspoon Worcestershire sauce

Combine fish with dairy sour cream, dip mix and worcestershire sauce. Chill thoroughly to blend flavors. Serve with assorted chips and crackers.

85 PARTY BALLS (cold)

For cold hors d' oeuvres, try these ingredients:

2 cups of flaked cooked trout or salmon
1 8 ounce package cream cheese, softened
1 tablespoon lemon juice
2 tsp. grated onion

1 tsp. prepared horseradish
¼ tsp. liquid smoke
½ cup chopped pecans
3 tablespoons snipped parsley

Drain and flake salmon, removing bones and skin. Combine salmon, cheese, lemon juice, onion, horseradish, ¼ tsp. salt, and liquid smoke, mix. Chill several hours. Combine pecans and parsley. Shape mixture into ball, roll in nut mixture. Chill and serve with crackers.

86 FISH BALL Appetizers (hot)

For hot hors d' oeuvres, use these ingredients:
2 cups cooked finely flaked fish (most any variety)
½ tsp. salt
½ tsp. dry mustard
1 tablespoon lemon juice
1 cup thick cream sauce (page 54, recipe #56)
1 tablespoon chopped parsley
½ tsp. onion juice

Mix and chill. Shape into balls. Fry at 375° in deep fat. Drain on paper. You can serve with cocktail sauce, or a sour cream onion dip.

87 WALLEYE SNACK-STACKS

Next time you entertain your bridge club, serve this surprise:
1 pound fresh fish fillets
1 10 ounce package frozen asparagus spears
¼ cup chopped onion
2 tablespoons butter
2 tablespoons all purpose flour
¼ tsp. dried basil leaves, crushed
1¼ cups milk
2 tablespoons, chopped, canned pimiento
3 English muffins, split, toasted and buttered

Cut fish into 6 pieces. Steam or poach fish until done. Cook asparagus according to directions on package and drain. Cook onion in butter till golden, and blend in flour, ½ tsp. salt and basil, add milk, cook and stir until thickened. Add pimiento and heat through.

To serve, place 2 muffin halves on each plate, top with fillets, then asparagus. Pour cream sauce oven stack-ups.

88 STEAMED CARP

Don't turn up your nose 'til you try it! More carp is eaten in this world than any other fish.

1 3 pound fresh carp
1 medium onion, sliced
2 sprigs parsley
1 bay leaf
3 whole peppercorns

Pour water into poacher or large skillet to depth of ½ inch. Add onion, parsley, bay leaf, peppercorns and salt. Bring to boiling. Place carp on a greased rack, set into skillet, cover and cook until it flakes easily (about 20 to 25 minutes). Drain and serve with Horseradish Sauce or Hollandaise Sauce.

89 FISH SLAW

Your family won't believe this one! But try it. You will need the following ingredients:

4 slices bacon
¼ cup chopped onion
⅓ cup vinegar
1 tsp. sugar
½ tsp. salt
Dash pepper
2 cups shredded cabbage
1 pound fish, cooked and flaked (2 cups) - any variety from walleye to salmon.

In skillet fry bacon til crisp. Drain bacon, reserving drippings. Crumble bacon, set aside. In same skillet cook onion in drippings 'til tender. Add vinegar, sugar, salt, and pepper, bring to boiling. Stir in cabbage and flaked fish. Cook, tossing lightly just until heated through. Turn into serving bowl and sprinkle top with reserved crumbled bacon.

90 GRILLED FISH SANDWICHES

Bored with the same old sandwiches? Here's an exciting variation:

1 pound any fish, cooked and flaked
¼ cup Thousand Island salad dressing
12 slices bread
6 slices process Swiss cheese
6 tablespoons butter
2 tsp. finely chopped onion

Combine flaked fish and dressing, spread on slices of bread. Place one slice of cheese on each and top with remaining bread. Blend butter and onion together. Spread on both sides of sandwiches. Grill until brown and cheese melts. Serve while hot.

TIPS ON CATCHING SUNFISH

- "Sunnies" are a favorite to eat and fun to catch. They seem to be hungry all the time; it is mostly a matter of locating them. Like crappies, they are found in schools (except during spawning time in early June.)
- Look for sunfish in shallow water in very early spring and again in early June when they are on their spawning beds. As the summer progresses, they will migrate to deeper waters - usually in or near weedbeds. Larger sunfish, in particular, can be found in 12 to 15 feet of water - sometimes twenty yards or more from the weedbeds.
- Because of their small mouths, it is necessary to use small hooks. Worms are the most reliable bait in summer, but when fishing through the ice, little jigs (feathered or tear drop) baited with "mousies" or wax worms are most effective.
- Surface fishing over weedbeds with a fly rod is great sport - particularly towards evening.
- For really big "sunnies" try a very small minnow or troll a miniature Lazy Ike or Flatfish with just a little angleworm on one or more of the hooks for flavor.
- Sunfish usually feed several feet off bottom. If perch are a bother, you are probably fishing a little too deep.

chapter X

THESE GO WELL WITH FISH

91 COURT BOUILLON

You can use this to poach fish in, as the base of fish soups and chowders, or to add to Hollandaise sauce when served with fish.

3 quarts water
1 tablespoon butter
1 tablespoon salt
2 tablespoons lemon juice and the sliced rind of the lemon
3 peppercorns
1 bay leaf
¼ cup sliced onion
1 piece celery
1 carrot.

Bring to a boil then cook over low heat for 20 minutes.

90 BEER SAUCE

Ingredients:

2# fillets (any kind)
5 oz. of shallot onions, finely cut and braised in butter
2 oz. of ginersnap crumbs
1 stalk celery, cut finely
Parsley

Put fish in a kettle and add the onions, celery, gingersnap crumbs, parsley and salt. Cover the whole with a bottle of beer and cook slowly until done. All alcohol evaporates from the mixture.

To prepare a sauce to use over the fish, remove the fish and cook the broth down to two-thirds of its volume. Strain, add 5 oz. of butter, beat lightly.

93 CUCUMBER SAUCE

1 medium cucumber (skin on) grated
2 tablespoons onion, chopped very fine
2 tablespoons vinegar
1 tablespoon chopped lettuce or parsley
¼ cup mayonnaise
½ cup sour cream
salt and pepper.

Remove seeds from cucumber and grate.
Blend all ingredients well; refrigerate.

94 COLESLAW[1]

1 medium or small head cabbage
1 medium or small onion
1 small green pepper (not essential)

Grate and mix together all of the above ingredients.
Dressing:

7/8 cup sugar
1 tablespoon salt
1 cup salad dressing
½ cup tarragon vinegar

Blend all of the salad ingredients together and stir into the cabbage mixture.

95 QUICK SALAD

1 head lettuce
½ cup mayonnaise
⅓ cup catsup
1 tomato, cut into wedges
croutons (optional)

This is an easy one that really goes well with fish. Remove the core of the head of lettuce and break the remainder of the head into small pieces. Blend the catsup into the mayonnaise, add to the lettuce, and toss. Arrange tomato wedges on top.

For a special touch, add croutons.

[1]Mrs. Harriet Dent, Staples, Minnesota.

6 3 BEAN SALAD

1 can green beans - drained
1 can yellow beans - drained
1 can kidney beans - drained
½ cup green pepper, chopped fine
½ cup onion, chopped fine
1 cup cider vinegar
1 tablespoon worchestershire sauce
1 teaspoon Bar B Q sauce
½ cup salad oil
¾ cup sugar
1 teaspoon salt
1 teaspoon pepper

Drain the three cans of beans and place them in a bowl. Stir in the green pepper and onion. Mix the oil, vinegar, and all other ingredients. Pour over the beans and mix well. Store in refrigerator in covered dish to be served the next day with fish.

7 BAKED BEANS (doctored from the can)

Serving for four:

1 2½# can (about 30 oz.) of pork and beans
2 pieces of thick bacon
½ cup brown sugar (or, ¼ cup molasses and ¼ cup brown sugar)
½ cup catsup
2 tablespoons mustard
a few pieces of green pepper
1 tablespoon chopped onion

Cut the bacon strips into half-inch pieces and fry over medium heat until light brown - not crisp. Place the pieces of bacon and a little of the grease in the bottom of a kettle. (Help the dishwashers by using the same kettle for frying the bacon as you will use for heating the beans.) Add the beans, brown sugar, catsup, mustard, onion, and green pepper. Stir and heat (medium). Simmer for at least fifteen minutes . . . the longer the better. Stir occasionally.

The key ingredients are brown sugar and catsup - so if you are short any or all of the other additives, do not hesitate to "doctor" the beans with just these two items. Molasses may be substituted for all or part of the brown sugar.

Beans are an excellent side dish with fish or meat and a good potato substitute.

98 VARIATIONS OF BOILED POTATOES

Peel and wash eight medium size potatoes (four servings). Cut the potatoes into two or three pieces so that they will cook more quickly. Place in pan, cover with water, add a tablespoon of salt, and boil until done (a table fork will easily penetrate the potatoes and go all the way through). Do not overcook so that the potatoes become mushy or fall apart. Drain the potatoes and put them back on the heat for just a few seconds. This will dry them and make them lighter. Serve with butter.

Small potatoes boiled whole and served with chopped parsley and melted butter are also a special treat.

Potatoes fresh from the garden in early summer have thin skins and may be boiled with their "jackets" on and served the same way. Wash them with special care before cooking.

For a special treat with fried fish, boil "new" potatoes just out of the garden in early summer and serve (mashed on the plate with a fork) with light cream (half and half) - generously sprinkled with chopped chives (grass onions). Let each person salt and pepper to taste.

99 HUSH PUPPIES

2 cups self rising white corn meal
1 small onion, chopped fine
1/4 cup green pepper, chopped fine
1 egg, beaten
3/4 cup milk

Combine corn meal, sugar, green pepper, and onion in a bowl. Combine milk and egg and stir into the ingredients in the bowl.

Drop large tablespoons of dough into hot fat (375°) and let fry until a golden brown.

100 HERRING SALAD (Sil Salad)

This is a favorite Smorgasbord item brought to this country by Scandinavian immigrants in the last century. The following ingredients are for 8 to 10 servings:

1 large salt herring
1 cup cooked beets, diced
1 1/4 cup cooked potatoes, diced
1 cup diced roast beef (or beef or ham)
1 pickle, finely chopped (medium - sweet)
1 1/2 apple, medium, peeled and diced

2 tablespoons vinegar
1 teaspoon sugar
1/8 teaspoon white pepper
1 hard boiled egg; cut white into strips, mash yolk
¼ cup whipping cream (whip) or ½ cup sour cream

Soak the herring in water overnight. Rinse, remove skin and bones.

Mix herring, diced beets, diced potatoes, diced meat, diced apple, chopped pickle and add vinegar, sugar, and pepper.

Turn out on a platter and garnish with mashed egg yolk in center with egg white strips arranged in a spiral around the yolk. You may also add parsley and small, cooked beets for decoration.

Serve with either whipped or sour cream. Some prefer to stir the cream into the salad before it is placed on the platter.

101 TARTAR SAUCES

WHITE

1 cup mayonnaise or salad dressing
¼ cup sweet pickle relish
1 tablespoon chopped onion (fine)

Stir the pickle relish and chopped onion into the mayonnaise.

RED

½ cup chili sauce
⅓ cup ketchup
⅓ cup prepared horseradish
1½ tsp. worchestershire sauce
¼ tsp. salt
2 tablespoons lemon juice
1/8 tsp. pepper
¼ cup minced celery

Combine all ingredients. Place in jar, cover and chill before serving. Makes 1½ cups.

GARNISHES FOR FRIED FISH

Lemon, lime or orange slices sprinkled with minced pimiento parsley or green pepper.

Grapefruit sections dusted with paprika.

Thick tomato slices topped with pickle relish or with thin lemon slices topped with slices of stuffed olives.

Canned pineapple slices, drained, topped with little haystacks of coleslaw.
Celery sticks or fans or cheese stuffed.
Cucumber slices, fluted and sprinkled with tarragon vinegar.
Pickled beet slices dotted with horseradish sauce.

Other Books by Duane R. Lund

Andrew, Youngest Lumberjack
A Beginner's Guide to Hunting and Trapping
A Kid's Guidebook to Fishing Secrets
Early Native American Recipes and Remedies
Fishing and Hunting Stories from The Lake of the Woods
Lake of the Woods, Yesterday and Today, Vol. 1
Lake of the Woods, Earliest Accounts, Vol. 2
Our Historic Boundary Waters
Our Historic Upper Mississippi
Tales of Four Lakes and a River
The Youngest Voyageur
White Indian Boy
Nature's Bounty for Your Table
The North Shore of Lake Superior, Yesterday and Today
101 Favorite Wild Rice Recipes
101 Favorite Mushroom Recipes
Camp Cooking, Made Easy and Fun
Sauces, Seasonings and Marinades for Fish and Wild Game
The Scandinavian Cookbook
Gourmet Freshwater Fish Recipes, Quick and Easy
101 Ways to Add to Your Income
The Indian Wars
Traditional Holiday Ethnic Recipes - collected all over the world
Entertainment Helpers, Quick and Easy

About the Author

- EDUCATOR (RETIRED, SUPERINTENDENT OF SCHOOLS, STAPLES, MINNESOTA);

- HISTORIAN (PAST MEMBER OF EXECUTIVE BOARD, MINNESOTA HISTORICAL SOCIETY); Past Member of BWCA and National Wilderness Trails Advisory Committees;

- TACKLE MANUFACTURER (PRESIDENT, LUND TACKLE CO.);

- WILDLIFE ARTIST, OUTDOORSMAN.